TAXATION (TX-UK)
(Finance Act 2022)

For June 2023 to March 2024 examination sittings

Pocket notes

KAPLAN
PUBLISHING

British library cataloguing-in-publication data

A catalogue record for this book is available from the British Library.

Published by:
Kaplan Publishing UK
Unit 2 The Business Centre
Molly Millars Lane
Wokingham
Berkshire
RG41 2QZ

ISBN 978-1-83996-171-7

© Kaplan Financial Limited, 2022

Printed and bound in Great Britain.

Contents

		Reference to Study text chapter	Page Number

Preface

These pocket notes contain the key points you need to know for the exam, presented in a unique visual way that makes revision easy and effective.

Written by experienced lecturers and authors, these pocket notes break down content into manageable chunks to maximise your concentration.

Throughout these notes you will find references to past questions including the name of the question in the Kaplan exam kit. These have been included to enable you to locate the questions in the exam kit. Please be aware that due to changes in the examination format in recent years, all questions have been adapted from their original format in order to be representative of the format and style of questions that you are likely to see in your TX examination. Therefore, there may be differences between the Kaplan examination version and the version available on the ACCA website, which will not have been updated to the current examination format.

Quality and accuracy are of the utmost importance to us so if you spot an error in any of our products, please send an email to mykaplanreporting@kaplan.com with full details, or follow the link to the feedback form in MyKaplan.

Our Quality Co-ordinator will work with our technical team to verify the error and take action to ensure it is corrected in future editions.

The examination

TX is assessed by a three hour computer based examination (CBE).

The exam will consist of 3 compulsory sections A, B and C.

Section A will be comprised of 15 objective test (OT) questions of 2 marks each.

Section B will be comprised of 3 objective test (OT) case questions with five OT questions worth 2 marks each linked to each case.

Section C will be comprised of one 10 mark and two 15 mark constructed response (long) questions.

One of the two 15 mark questions will focus on income tax (syllabus area B) and the other on corporation tax (syllabus area E).

The section A questions, section B questions and the 10 mark section C question can cover any areas of the syllabus.

Aims and capabilities

Aim of the exam

To develop knowledge and skills relating to the tax system as applicable to individuals, single companies, and groups of companies.

Main capabilities

On successful completion of this exam candidates should be able to:

- explain the operation and scope of the tax system and the obligations of taxpayers and/or their agents and the implications of non-compliance

- explain and compute the income tax liabilities of individuals and the effect of national insurance contributions (NICs) on employees, employers and the self-employed

- explain and compute the chargeable gains arising on individuals

- explain and compute the inheritance tax liabilities of individuals

- explain and compute the corporation tax liabilities of individual companies and groups of companies

- explain and compute the effects of value added tax (VAT) on incorporated and unincorporated businesses.

The keys to success in TX

The TX exam is divided into three different sections, requiring the application of different skills to be successful.

Spend time reading the exam carefully, paying particular attention to sections B and C, where questions will be based on longer scenarios than the 2 mark OTs in section A.

- Divide the time you spend on questions in proportion to the marks on offer.

- One suggestion for this examination is to allocate 1.8 minutes to each mark available (180 minutes/100 marks), so a 10 mark question should be completed in approximately 18 minutes.

Section A

Applying the timing principle of 1.8 minutes per mark for TX means that 15 objective test (OT) questions (30 marks) should take 54 minutes.

Work steadily. Rushing leads to careless mistakes and questions are designed to include answers which result from careless mistakes.

If you don't know the answer, eliminate those options you know are incorrect and see if the answer becomes more obvious.

Remember that only one answer to an OT question can be right and there is no negative marking for an incorrect answer.

After you have eliminated any options that you know to be wrong, if you are still unsure, guess.

Section B

Each case has five 2 mark OT questions linked to it, meaning that each case is worth 10 marks in total. You should therefore spend 18 minutes (10 x 1.8 minutes) tackling each case.

Read the information relating to each case carefully.

Firstly, identify any OT questions that can be answered without significant workings and attempt these. Use your remaining time to attempt the OT questions that require workings.

The above guidance for section A is equally valid for the section B OT questions.

Section C

Always show workings in questions.

Always state any assumptions you make if you do not understand what the question is asking.

Learn and follow the pro formas for computational questions.

Adopt a logical approach and cross reference workings to the main computation to keep your answer tidy.

All sections

Don't skip parts of the syllabus in your studies. The TX exam has 33 different questions that contribute to your overall mark so the examination can cover a very broad selection of the syllabus each sitting.

Spend time learning the rules and definitions.

Read the TX examining team's articles released in Student Accountant in the months up to your examination date. These give clues as to the areas that may be covered.

Practise plenty of questions to improve your ability to apply the techniques and perform the calculations.

Don't panic if you realise that you've answered a question incorrectly. Getting one question wrong will not mean the difference between passing and failing.

In the exam...

- Make sure you take a spare calculator.

- Decide the order in which to attempt the sections and stick to your plan.

- Work out the length of time you have to complete each question.

- Attempt all of the questions.

- Missing out questions makes it harder for you to achieve success – you still have to gain 50 marks!

- At the end of your time allocation, move on to the next question; if you have spare time at the end you can go back to any unfinished questions.

- Try to spend the last five minutes reading through your answers and making any additions or corrections.

- Be sure you understand how to use the CBE software before you start the examination. If in doubt, ask the assessment centre staff to explain it to you.

- Questions are displayed on screen and answers are entered using a keyboard and a mouse.

1

Income tax: basic computation, investment and property income

In this chapter

- Tax year.
- Taxable income.
- Exempt income.
- Pro forma – income tax computation.
- Reliefs.
- Personal allowance.
- Child benefit tax charge.
- Calculating income tax.
- Tax rates.
- Tax deducted at source.
- Property income.
- Joint income.
- Investment income.
- Residence.

Tax year

- An individual's taxable income is taxed in respect of a tax year.
- Runs from 6th April to following 5th April.

Tax year 2022/23: 6 April 2022 to 5 April 2023.

Taxable income

Taxable income	Basis of assessment
Profits from a trade/profession/vocation	Tax adjusted trading profits of the accounts ending in the current tax year
Interest received from UK sources	
Income from employment	Income received in the tax year
Dividend income	
Property income	Income received in the tax year is the default basis (accruals basis is used in certain circumstances)

Income taxed at different income tax rates
depending on type of income:

Non-savings	Savings	Dividends
↓	↓	↓
Employment income	Interest income	Dividend income
Trading profits		
Property income		

Income must be included in computation
gross.

Exam focus

Use the following income tax pro forma to ensure that income tax is calculated at the correct rates on different sources of income.

Exempt income

Main examples:

- Premium bond prizes.
- Betting/gambling winnings.
- Returns on NS&I certificates.
- Income received from ISAs.
- Repayment interest (interest on tax repayments).

Key Point

Any exempt income should be:

- excluded in the income tax computation
- but noted as exempt in section C exam answers.

Pro forma – Income tax computation – 2022/23

	Non-savings £	Savings £	Dividends £	Total £
Trading profits	X			X
Employment income	X			X
Property income	X			X
Pension income	X			X
Interest income		X		X
Dividend income			X	X
Total income	X	X	X	X
Less: Reliefs	(X)			(X)
Net income	X	X	X	X
Less: Personal Allowance (PA)	(12,570)			(12,570)
Taxable income	X	X	X	X

Income tax computation

	£
Non-savings income x 20/40/45%	X
Savings income x 0/20/40/45% (Note)	X
Dividend income x 0/8.75/33.75/39.35% (Note)	X
Income tax liability	X
Less: PAYE	(X)
Income tax payable	X

The appropriate rate of tax depends on the level of taxable income:

Basic rate band limit	= £37,700
Higher rate band limit	= £150,000

Note: Savings income falling into the first £5,000 of taxable income is taxed at 0% (not 20%).

A savings nil rate band of £1,000 and £500 is available to basic and higher rate tax payers respectively.

A dividend nil rate band of £2,000 is available to all taxpayers.

Exam focus

Exam kit questions in this area:

OT case (section B) question:

- Philip and Charles

Constructed response (section C) questions:

- Patience
- Richard Tryer
- Petula
- John Beach
- Dill
- Sam, Tam and Uma
- Kagan
- Kioni
- Jade

Reliefs

- Reliefs are an allowable deduction from the total income of an individual, subject to a maximum amount.

- Main examples:

    - Qualifying interest

        Employees:
        interest on loans to purchase plant and machinery for use in employment

        Partners:
        Interest on loans to purchase a share in a partnership or to contribute capital/loan to a partnership

    - Trading losses (Chapter 7).

- **Maximum amount of relief** deductible from total income is the **greater of**:

    - £50,000, or

    - 25% of adjusted total income.

Note that the maximum restriction will only be examined in the context of loss relief (see Chapter 7).

Personal allowance (PA)

- Available to all individuals.
- £12,570 for 2022/23.
- Deducted from net income to give taxable income.
- Lost if not used in the year.

Reduction of PA – higher rate taxpayers

- If adjusted net income (ANI) > £100,000:
  - reduce PA by:
    50% x (ANI – £100,000)
- If ANI > £125,140:
  - no PA
- Effective rate of tax on income between £100,000 to £125,140: 60%

- ANI is calculated as:

	£
Net income (per IT comp)	X
Less: Gross gift aid donations	(X)
Less: Gross personal pension contributions	(X)
ANI	X

Exam focus

Exam kit questions in this area:

OT case (section B) questions:

- Philip and Charles

Constructed response (section C) questions:

- Petula
- John Beach
- Dill

KAPLAN PUBLISHING

Marriage Allowance (Transferable amount)

- A spouse or civil partner can elect to transfer a fixed amount of the PA to the other spouse/civil partner.

- This is known as the marriage allowance (MA).

- Neither spouse/civil partner may be a higher or additional rate taxpayer.

Key Point

Electing for the MA will be beneficial provided the transferor spouse/civil partner does not fully utilise the PA but the recipient spouse/civil partner does, so that the total income tax liability of the couple is reduced.

Method:

- The fixed amount of PA to transfer = £1,260 for 2022/23.

- There is no provision for transferring less than this amount.

- Relief is given by reducing the recipient's income tax liability by a maximum of £252 (i.e. £1,260 x 20% BR income tax).

Child benefit tax charge

A child benefit charge arises where:

- an individual receives child benefit, and
- that individual, or the individual's spouse/ civil partner, have adjusted net income (ANI) > £50,000.

ANI = as for the restriction of the PA.

Income	Tax charge
£50,000 – £60,000	1% of child benefit for each £100 of income over £50,000
Over £60,000	The amount of child benefit received

Both the appropriate percentage and the tax charge are rounded down to the nearest whole number.

Where the charge applies the taxpayer must:

- complete a tax return
- pay the charge through the self-assessment system.

The tax charge can be avoided by choosing not to claim child benefit.

Exam focus

Exam kit questions in this area:

Constructed response (section C) questions:

- Amanda

Calculating income tax

(1) Dividends, savings income and non-savings income need to be totalled separately.

(2) To ensure that tax is saved at the highest rates, reliefs and the PA should be deducted from:

- non-savings income
- then savings income
- then dividends.

(3) Order of calculation

Tax should be calculated in the same order:

- non-savings income
- then savings income
- then dividends.

Tax rates

- Different tax rates apply depending on the amount and type of income.

	Non-savings	Savings	Dividends
Basic rate band (first £37,700)	20%	20% (Note)	8.75% (Note)
Higher rate band (£37,701 – £150,000)	40%	40%	33.75%
Additional rate band (over £150,000)	45%	45%	39.35%

Note: If savings income falls into the first £5,000 of taxable income, it is taxed at 0% (not 20%).

A savings nil rate band is available as follows

- Basic rate taxpayers £1,000
- Higher rate taxpayers £500

All taxpayers are entitled to a £2,000 dividend nil rate band.

Pension contributions

- Personal pensions

  Relief for contributions paid by an individual into a personal pension scheme, is given as follows:

  - Paid net of basic rate tax (20%)
  - Basic and higher rate bands extended by the gross amount: (amount paid x 100/80).

- Occupational pensions

  - Contributions deducted from employee's gross pay before PAYE is applied.

Charitable giving

Tax relief is available as follows:

- Gift aid scheme:
  - Paid net of basic rate tax (20%).
  - Basic and higher rate bands extended by the gross amount: (amount paid x 100/80).
- Payroll deduction scheme
  - Donations deducted from employee's gross pay before PAYE is applied.

Effect of extending bands

Income equivalent to gross personal pension contributions (PPC) and/or gross gift aid donations is

- taxed at 20% rather than 40% (if higher rate taxpayer) and in addition
- taxed at 40% rather than 45% (if an additional rate taxpayer).

This increases the amount of income taxed at a lower rate as opposed to a higher rate of tax.

Reduction of PA

In addition, remember that:

Gross PPCs and gift aid donations = also deducted from net income to arrive at ANI when comparing with the income limit for the reduction of the PA.

Exam focus

Exam kit questions in this area:

Constructed response (section C) questions

- Patience
- Richard Tryer
- John Beach
- Robinette
- Kioni

Tax deducted at source

- If tax deducted at source i.e. PAYE exceeds the income tax liability, the excess is repayable.

Property income

- Taxes income from land and property.
- The cash basis is the default basis in the TX examination. In certain circumstances the accruals basis is used.
- Calculation of profits:

	£
Rental income received	X
Less: Related expenses paid	(X)
Taxable income	X

- Expenditure is deductible if it is incurred 'wholly and exclusively' for the purposes of the letting (e.g. repairs, insurance, agents' fees).
- Interest paid = allowable deduction for non-residential property.

- Interest paid for residential property
  - Finance costs not deductible, but basic rate tax relief deduction from income tax liability instead.
- If a property is let furnished, the cost of replacement domestic items (i.e. not the original acquisition) is an allowable deduction.
- Where there is more than one property the profits and losses from each property are aggregated.
- Taxed as non-savings income at:
  - 20%, 40% or 45%
- Property losses
  - for individuals, can only be carried forward against future property income.

Exam focus

Exam kit questions in this area:

Constructed response (section C) questions:

- Patience
- Richard Tryer
- Tonie
- Kat

Premiums for granting a short lease

Where a premium is paid on the grant of a short lease (≤ 50 years):

- Landlord is taxed on property income of:

	£
Premium	X
Less: 2% x premium x (n – 1)	(X)
Taxable for landlord	Y

where

n = number of years of lease.

Alternative calculation:

$$= \text{Premium} \times \left(\frac{51 - n}{50} \right)$$

Furnished holiday lettings (FHL)

- Taxed as property income but:
  - treated as arising from a single and separate trade.

- Advantages:
  - Business asset for CGT rollover relief, gift holdover relief and business asset disposal relief.
  - Relevant earnings for pensions relief.
  - Deduction available on a paid basis for P&M including furniture when using the cash basis.
  - Capital allowances on all P&M including furniture when using the accruals basis.
  - Finance costs deductible from FHL income.

- Any losses made on a qualifying FHL property may only be set against profits from other qualifying FHL properties:
    - firstly in the same tax year
    - then carried forward against future profits from FHL properties only.
- Conditions:
    - Let furnished on commercial basis.
    - Available to let for ≥ 210 days in the year.
    - Actually let for ≥ 105 days in the year.
    - Not let for periods of long-term occupation (occupied by same person > 31 days) in excess of 155 days in a year.

Rent-a-room relief

- Furnished room in a main domestic residence.
- Gross rents ≤ £7,500
    - exempt, unless elect for loss.
- Gross rents > £7,500
    - normal property income calculation unless elect for excess over £7,500 to be taxed (with no deduction for expenses).

Exam focus

Exam kit question in this area:

Constructed response (section C) questions:

- Petula
- Tonie

Joint income

- Applies to married couples and civil partnerships.
- Normal assumption = 50/50 split.

Can elect for income to be taxed according to actual percentage ownership.

Investment income

ISAs
(two separate investments)

Cash ISA

Stocks and shares ISA

Maximum Investment per tax year

£20,000

Accrued income scheme

Applies to individuals holding gilts with a total nominal value in excess of £5,000.

- Gains made on gilts by individuals are exempt.

- Without the scheme, interest accrued up to the date of sale would increase the value of the gilt and be included as part of the exempt gain.

- When the accrued income scheme applies, the **interest accrued up to the date of sale** is treated as **savings income** for the individual selling the gilt.

- Similarly, an individual who buys a gilt from a previous holder, can deduct from the first interest receipt, any interest received which legally is taxable income of the previous owner.

Exam focus

Exam kit questions in this area:

Constructed response (section C) questions:

- Poppy
- Petula
- Tonie

Residence

- All individuals resident in the UK = taxed on their **worldwide income** (UK and overseas).

Key Point

Knowledge of the residency definition is important. However in computational questions, the individual will always be:

- resident in the UK, and
- taxed on worldwide income.

Definition

An individual is resident in the UK for a tax year if they:

- do not meet one of the **automatic non-UK residence tests**, and
- meet one of the **automatic UK residence tests**, or
- meet the required number of the **sufficient ties tests**.

Resident in UK?

Automatic non-UK residency tests	Automatic UK residency tests	Sufficient ties tests

Automatic non-UK residency tests

Individual in UK in **tax year** less than
- **16 days**, or
- **46 days** and not UK R in any of last 3 years, or
- **91 days** and works FT abroad

Automatic UK residency tests

Individual automatically UK R if:
- In UK **183 days** in tax year, or
- Only home in UK, or
- Work FT in UK

Sufficient ties tests

1 Close family in the UK
   – Spouse/Civil partner/minor child
2 Accommodation in UK
   – used in tax year
3 Substantive work in UK
4 Days in UK in last two tax years
   – › 90 days in either year
5 Country tie – Most time spent in UK

Previously resident in UK
= UK R in one of last 3 years
_____
Consider **all five** ties

See tax tables in exam

Not previously resident in UK
= not UK R in any of last 3 years
_____
Consider **first four** ties

Application of sufficient ties test

Days spent in the UK	Previously resident (Leaver)	Not previously resident (Arriver)
Less than 16 days	Automatically **not** UK resident	Automatically **not** UK resident
16 to 45 days	Resident if: 4 UK ties (or more)	Automatically **not** UK resident
46 to 90 days	Resident if: 3 UK ties (or more)	Resident if: 4 UK ties
91 to 120 days	Resident if: 2 UK ties (or more)	Resident if: 3 UK ties (or more)
121 to 182 days	Resident if: 1 UK tie (or more)	Resident if: 2 UK ties (or more)
183 or more days	Automatically resident	Automatically resident

Application of sufficient ties test

The above table is included in the tax rates and allowances provided to you in the examination. No other information relating to residence is included in the tax rates and allowances.

Exam focus

Sections A and B will almost certainly include some questions on income tax. In addition, one of the questions in section C will focus on income tax for 15 marks, and the 10 mark section C question may also include income tax aspects.

It is highly likely, therefore, that a question will involve the calculation of income tax liability or payable.

It is important that you familiarise yourself with the various types of income, along with the order in which they are taxed, and also how to apply the different rates of tax for interest and dividends.

As with all areas of the TX syllabus, question practice is the key to success and is invaluable when it comes to taxing the different sources of income at the correct tax rates accurately under time pressure.

Exam kit questions in this area:

Constructed response (section C) questions:

- Dill
- Auy Man and Bim Men
- Tonie

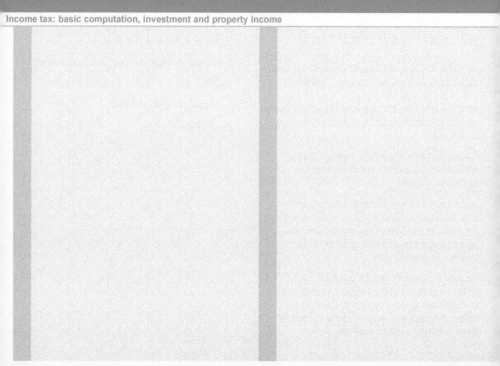

Employment income

In this chapter

- Employment v self-employment.
- Employment income.
- Benefits.
- Living accommodation.
- Company cars.
- Fuel benefit.
- Company vans.
- Beneficial loans.
- Use and transfer of assets.

Employment v self-employment

An employee works under a **contract of service** and a self-employed person under a **contract for services**.

The main criteria to look at when deciding between the two are:

- Hours
- Integration
- Source of work
- Control
- Holidays
- Obligation
- Risk/Reward
- Equipment
- Substitutes

Key Point

Remember: HIS CHORES

Employment income

Basis of assessment

- Earnings are taxed on the receipts basis

    - Usually amounts are taxable for the tax year in which they are paid regardless of when earned.

    - An earlier 'received' date can apply for directors:

        - the date when the earnings are credited in the company's books (internal accounts) as payable to the director

        - the end of the accounting period, where earnings are determined before the end of that period

        - the date when earnings are determined, if after the end of the accounting period.

Employment income pro forma

	£
Salary/wages	X
Bonus	X
Benefits	X
	X
Less: Allowable deductions	(X)
Employment income	X

Allowable deductions

- Expenses specifically allowable:
  - contributions to occupational pension schemes
  - subscriptions to professional bodies
  - charitable donations under a payroll deduction scheme.
- Travel expenses are deductible if they are incurred necessarily in the performance of the duties of employment.
- Other expenses are deductible if they are incurred **wholly, exclusively and necessarily in the performance** of those duties.

Approved Mileage Allowance Payments (AMAP)

- Apply where an employee is paid a mileage allowance by the employer for using the employee's own car for business travel.

The AMAP rates are included in the tax rates and allowances provided to you in the examination.

Exam focus

Exam kit questions in this area:

Constructed response (section C) questions:

- Dill
- John Beach
- Tonie
- Robinette

Benefits

- There are two main categories:
  (1) Exempt benefits
  (2) Taxable benefits

Exempt benefits

- Trivial benefits (except vouchers) with a cost to the employer of no more than £50 per gift and not in recognition of services provided

- Employer's contribution to pension scheme

- Canteen facilities provided for all employees

- Employee relocation costs up to £8,000

- Works buses for home to work travel

- Job-related accommodation

- One mobile telephone for private use per employee

- Workplace nurseries for childcare

- Up to £6 per week towards additional household costs where the employee works from home

- Annual staff parties costing no more than £150 per person per annum

- Car parking space at or near place of work
- Reimbursement of expenses for working away from home:
  - £5 per night if in the UK, and
  - £10 per night if overseas
- Recreational or sporting facilities available to all employees and not to the public generally
- Cheap loans provided loan is ≤ £10,000 throughout the tax year
- Medical expenses of up to £500 per employee per tax year to enable an employee to return to work following an absence due to injury or ill health.
- A bicycle / cycle safety equipment provided for employee to cycle to and from work (other private use also allowed), if available on same terms to all employees.

Key Point

Any exempt benefits should be:

- excluded in the employment income computation
- but noted as exempt in section C examination answers.

Taxable benefits

General principles

When calculating the taxable amount for any benefit consider:

* Payments made by the employee for the benefit = deductible

* Time apportionment when the benefit is only available for part of the tax year.

	£
Benefit calculated for tax year	X
Less: Periods when unavailable	(X)
Less: Employee contributions	(X)
Taxable benefit	X

Benefit	Taxable amount
Cash vouchers	Cash which voucher can be exchanged for
Non-cash vouchers	Cost to employer
Credit cards	All items purchased for personal use (not interest or card charges)
Payment by employer of an employee's liability	Amount paid by employer (e.g. home telephone bill)
Living accommodation	Up to three components (see below)
Cars & fuel	Based on CO_2 emissions (see later)
Vans	Flat rate scale charge
Interest-free/low interest loans	Based on official rate of interest
Assets loaned	Based on 20% of market value of asset when first provided
Gift of new asset	Cost to employer
Other	Cost to the employer, or Marginal cost to the employer for 'in-house' benefits

Living accommodation

Benefit	Taxable amount	Job-related accommodation
Basic charge	Higher of: • Annual value • Rent paid by employer	Exempt
Expensive accommodation charge (where employer owns property and cost is > £75,000)	(Cost – £75,000) x ORI ORI = official rate of interest (provided in the examination)	Exempt
Ancillary services: • Use of furniture • Living expenses (e.g. heating, electricity, decorating)	 20% x market value when first provided Cost to employer	Same as for non-job related accommodation except: Maximum total benefit restricted to 10% of other employment income

Key Point

- Where the employer rents the accommodation there can never be an expensive accommodation charge.

- For the expensive accommodation charge:

  Cost = Acquisition cost of the property **plus** capital improvements up to the **start** of the tax year.

  If the property is occupied by the employee more than 6 years after it was acquired by the employer:

  - substitute the acquisition cost with the market value at the date the property was first occupied by the employee.

Job-related accommodation

Definition

Accommodation which is:

- necessary for proper performance of employee's duties, or

- provided for the better performance of duties and it is customary to provide such accommodation, or

- provided as part of special security arrangements because of a specific threat to the employee's security.

Exam focus

Exam kit questions in this area:

Constructed response (section C) question

- Richard Tryer

- Jason

- Alfred and Amaia

- Amanda

Company cars

- Benefit arises where an employer provides a car and it is available for private use.
- Benefit:

| Relevant % | x | List price of car (when new) |

Petrol/diesel cars
- 51-54g/km = 15%
- 55g/km = 16%
- +1% each 5g/km > 55g/km
- 4% supplement for diesel cars that do not meet the RDE2 standard
- 37% cap overall

Hybrid-electric cars - based on electric range
- 130 miles or more = 2%
- 70 to 129 miles = 5%
- 40 to 69 miles = 8%
- 30 to 39 miles = 12%
- Less than 30 miles = 14%

Electric cars = 2%

- Include extras
- Reduced by employee contribution to capital cost (max £5,000)

- If car unavailable for part of the year:
  - Proportional reduction in benefit only if car unavailable for > 30 days.
- Employee contributions for private use
  - reduce taxable benefit.
- Cars only used for business (e.g. pool cars)
  - no taxable benefit.
- Car benefit figure includes all running costs of the car (i.e. there is no additional benefit for insurance, services, etc. paid for by the employer).

Exam focus

Exam kit questions in this area:

Constructed response (section C) questions

- Richard Feast
- Richard Tryer
- Petula
- Jason
- Sam, Tam and Uma
- Poppy

Fuel benefit

- Where fuel provided for private use of a company car.
- Benefit:

Relevant % x £25,300

- Relevant % = same as car benefit
- No benefit if:
    - Employee pays for all fuel for private use.
    - Fuel is only provided for business use.
- If private fuel is permanently withdrawn the benefit is proportionately reduced.

Exam focus

Exam kit questions in this area:

Constructed response (section C) question:

- Richard Tryer

Key Point

There is no reduction in the fuel benefit where an employee only partially reimburses the cost of private fuel.

Company vans

- Flat rate scale charge of £3,600 p.a.
- Additional benefit of £688 p.a. if private fuel is provided.
- No benefit if private use is insignificant or limited to ordinary commuting between home and work.
- Van with zero CO_2 emissions - no van private use benefit, no fuel benefit

Beneficial loans

Where an employee is provided with an interest-free or cheap loan:

	£
Interest on outstanding balance at ORI	X
Less: Interest actually paid	(X)
Taxable benefit	X

ORI = official rate of interest
(will be given in the examination)

For FA2022 examination sittings, ORI = 2%

Exam focus

Exam kit questions in this area:

Constructed response (section C) questions:

- Patience
- Daniel, Francine and Gregor
- John Beach
- Dill

- Jason

Two methods of calculating the benefit:

- Average method
- Precise method.

Average method

- Average balance for the year is calculated by:

$$\frac{L_1 + L_2}{2} \times \frac{M}{12}$$

- L_1 loan outstanding at the beginning of the tax year or date when first loaned if loaned during tax year

- L_2 loan outstanding at the end of the tax year or date fully repaid if repaid in full during tax year

- M Number of whole months during which the loan was outstanding in the tax year.

Precise method

- ORI charged on a daily basis on the actual amount outstanding (calculated on monthly basis in the examination).
- Taxpayer or HMRC allowed to elect for the precise method to be used.

Exceptions

- No benefit if:
  - total of loans outstanding throughout the tax year is ≤ £10,000, or
  - loans are made on ordinary commercial terms (i.e. same terms as to the public).

Exam focus

The benefit should be calculated using both methods in the examination unless the question states otherwise.

Use and transfer of assets

Use of asset

- 20% of market value of asset when first made available.
- 20% rule does not apply to private use of cars, vans and accommodation provided by an employer.

Transfer of asset

New asset

- Benefit = Cost to employer

(continued on next page)

Used asset:

- Benefit is greater of:

	£
– Market value at time of transfer	X
Less: Amount paid by employee	(X)
	X

and

– Market value when first used	X
Less: Amount charged as	
benefit over period of use	(X)
Less: Amount paid by employee	(X)
	X

- These rules do not apply to the transfer of:
  - a used car or van
  - bicycles provided for work.

  The benefit in this instance is the market value at the date of transfer.

Exam focus

It is necessary to have a clear grasp of the benefit calculation rules.

Note that the TX examining team may also provide superfluous information such as the actual car running costs incurred by the employer. You are expected to know that the car benefit covers all running costs (except car fuel).

The better you know the rules the less likely it is that misleading points will distract you.

3

Income from self-employment

In this chapter

- Badges of trade.
- Trading income.
- Adjustment of trading profit.
- Disallowable expenditure.
- Trading income not included in the accounts.
- Non-trading income.
- Expenditure not charged in the accounts but allowable trading expenditure.
- Cash basis for small businesses.
- Flat rate expense deduction.

Badges of trade

- Factors used to determine if an activity constitutes trading or an investment.
- The outcome of this decision will affect whether the income is taxed as a capital gain or trading income.
- Original six badges of trade:

Test		Consider
Subject matter	S	Is asset purchased for personal use, an investment or for trading? Some assets are more normally purchased for personal reasons/investment (e.g. painting) than for trading purposes (e.g. toilet rolls)
Ownership period	O	Brief period of ownership indicates trading
Frequency of transactions	F	Repeated similar transactions indicate trading
Improvements	I	Work to make asset more marketable may indicate trading
Reason for sale	R	Forced sale to raise cash indicates not trading
Motive	M	Intention to profit from transaction indicates trading

Also consider:

Test		Consider
Finance	F	Was a loan taken out to finance the purchase which will need to be repaid on sale? If yes, then this may indicate trading.
Acquisition method	A	An asset acquired via a gift or inheritance indicates not trading
Existence of Similar Trading Transactions	S T	Similarities to an existing trade indicate trading

Key Point

Remember: SOFIRM and FAST

Be prepared to use the badges of trade to determine whether a particular transaction would be classed as a trading activity.

Trading income

The profits of an unincorporated trader arising from a trade are taxed as trading income.

To determine the taxable profits:

(1) Adjust the net profit per the accounts for tax purposes.

(2) Apply the basis of assessment rules to determine the profits taxable in a tax year (Chapter 5).

Adjustment of trading profit

The starting point is the net profit per the business' financial accounts.

Need to adjust this figure for items that are disallowable for tax purposes and income that is not taxable as trading income.

Pro forma – Tax adjusted trading profit

	£	£
Net profit per accounts	X	
Add: Expenditure not allowed for taxation purposes	X	
Expenditure allowable for taxation purposes	0	
Taxable trading profit not credited in the accounts	X	
Less: Expenditure not charged in the accounts but allowable for the purposes of taxation		X
Income included in the accounts that is not taxable as trading profit		X
Capital allowances (see Chapter 4)		X
	X	Y
	(Y)	
Tax adjusted trading profit	X	

The tax adjusted profit computation is a regularly tested topic for the TX examination. It is essential that you learn the pro forma for adjusting trading profits and practise questions in this area.

Exam kit questions in this area:

OT case (section B) question:

- Greenzone Ltd

Constructed response (section C) questions:

- Richard Feast
- Alfred and Amaia
- Last-Orders Ltd
- E-Commerce plc
- Lucky Ltd
- Retro Ltd
- Jump Ltd
- Clueless Ltd
- Long Ltd and Road Ltd

- Harbour Ltd
- Mooncake Ltd

Disallowable expenditure

- General rule:
  only expenditure incurred **wholly** and **exclusively** for the **purposes of the trade** is allowable.

- Adjust for proprietor's private expenditure.
  Examples:

  - Income tax payments

  - NICs

  - Private element of expenses such as car expenses and telephone bills.

- Disallow the proprietor's salary/drawings.

Salaries/private expenses of employees are allowable.

KAPLAN PUBLISHIN

Disallowable expenditure – examples

Disallowable	Allowable
Capital expenditure	
Depreciation, profit/loss on sale of assets, improvements	Repairs
Legal fees	
If relate to capital item (e.g. purchase of a building) Exceptions: • costs of renewing short lease (≤ 50 years) • costs of defending title to an asset • cost of raising loan finance	If relate to revenue item (e.g. collection of trade receivables)
Fines/penalties	
VAT penalties, fine for breaking health & safety regulations	Parking fine incurred by employee (but not proprietor/owner)
Donations	
To national charities/political parties Gift aid donations	Small amounts to local charities – effectively advertising

Disallowable	Allowable
Entertaining	
Customers, suppliers	Staff
Impairment losses	
Write off of non-trade debt (e.g. loan to a customer)	Write off of trade debt
	Allowance for impairment of trade receivables
Interest payable	
Late payment interest re overdue tax	Interest paid on trading loans (e.g. bank overdraft, hire purchase contracts)

Car leasing costs

Part of leasing/hire charge is disallowed for high emission cars (CO_2 emissions are more than 50g/km).

Disallowed amount = (15% x leasing costs or hire charge).

Gifts to customers

Only allowable if:

- incorporates conspicuous advertisement for the business, and
- total cost per donee is ≤ £50 per annum, and
- does not consist of food, drink or tobacco.

Gifts to staff

Allowable.

Trading income not included in the accounts

- Most common example is goods taken for own use by the proprietor.
- For tax purposes the trader is treated as making a sale at the normal selling price.
- If no entries have been made in the accounts for the transaction
    - add back the sale price.
- If the trader has already added back the cost of the goods in the accounts
    - only add back the profit element of the transaction.

Non-trading income

- Deduct income that is taxed in another way or is not taxable.
- This income is deducted from the net profit per the accounts.

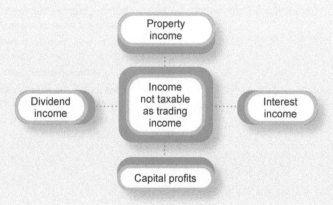

Expenditure not charged in the accounts but allowable trading expenditure

- Capital allowances.
- Any business expense paid for by the proprietor (e.g. business calls on a home telephone).
- The annual deduction for premium paid by tenant for grant of short lease on business premises:

$$\text{Deduction} = \frac{Y}{\text{Period of lease}}$$

Y = premium taxable on landlord as property income calculated as follows:

	£
Premium	X
Less: 2% x (n – 1) x premium	(X)
	Y

Where n = duration of lease in years

Alternative calculation:

$$P \times \left(\frac{51 - n}{50} \right)$$

Exam focus

It is highly likely that an adjustment of profit question will feature in your exam.

The presentation of the question is usually in the form of an extract from the statement of profit or loss, complete with notes and a breakdown of each of the different types of income and expense.

The way to tackle these questions is to carefully work through the scenario, making a note of any disallowable expenditure or non-trading income.

Make sure you don't forget to include the obvious adjustments, such as depreciation and capital allowances.

If you are in doubt as to how to treat a particular item, use the basic "wholly and exclusively" test.

If still in doubt, make an educated assumption of how to treat the item and state your assumption in your answer.

Then lay out the pro forma, starting with the net profit figure, and systematically work through all the items of expenditure and income in the question, marking them off as you go along.

By using the pro forma, and sticking to this logical approach, you will ensure you don't miss anything out of the question.

For section C questions, note that any allowable items must still be shown in your answer in the order they appear in the question, and shown as an add back adjustment of zero (0).

Similarly, all income should be listed and non-trading income adjusted for.

It is important to use the pro forma in section C questions to make your answer as clear as possible for the marker.

Cash basis for small businesses

- Cash basis = calculating profits/losses on the basis of cash received and cash paid in the period of account (instead of normal accruals basis).
- Optional.
- Only available to unincorporated businesses (i.e. sole traders and partnerships) – not companies and LLPs.
- Business must have cash receipts ≤ £150,000.
- Can continue to account on cash basis until cash receipts are > £300,000.

Exam focus

It should be assumed that the cash basis does **not** apply **unless** it is specifically mentioned in the question.

Under the cash basis:

- accounts can be prepared to any date in the year
- there is no distinction between capital and revenue expenditure re plant, machinery and equipment for tax purposes
- the flat rate expense deduction for car expenses (see below) will always be claimed instead of capital allowances in the TX examination.

Advantages

- Simpler accounting.
- Profit taxed when realised and cash available to pay.

Disadvantages

- Losses can only be carried forward.

Flat rate expense deduction

Any unincorporated business (whether or not they are using the cash basis) can:

- opt to use flat rate expense adjustments
- to replace the calculation of actual costs incurred in respect of those expenses.

Exam focus

However in the TX examination:

- flat rate expenses will only be examined where the business has chosen the cash basis, and
- if the cash basis applies, the use of flat rate expenses will be assumed to also apply.

Calculate the profit under the cash basis by doing a revised profit computation, rather than adjusting the net profit (as you would under the accruals basis).

Type of expense	Flat rate expense adjustment
Car expenses	Allowable deduction = amount using the AMAP rates of 45p and 25p per mile (Note 1)
Private use of part of a commercial building (e.g. accommodation in a small hotel or guest house)	Adjustment = fixed amount based on the number of occupants (Note 2). Covers: private use of household goods and services, rent, food and utilities

Notes: If required:

1. AMAP rates are included in the tax rates and allowances provided to you in the examination.

2. Fixed amount will be provided within the question.

Private element of other expenses (e.g. council tax and rates) = adjusted for as normal.

4

Capital allowances

In this chapter

- Introduction.
- Plant and machinery.
- Pro forma – Capital allowances computation for unincorporated businesses.
- The allowances (See Chapter 10 for differences for companies).
- The special rate pool.
- The small pool WDA.
- Short life assets (SLA).
- Private use assets.
- Business cessation.
- VAT.
- Approach to computational questions for unincorporated businesses.
- Effect of accounting period length for unincorporated businesses.
- Structures and buildings allowances.

Introduction

- Depreciation is disallowable for tax purposes.
- Tax relief for capital expenditure on certain types of expenditure is given through capital allowances.
- Capital allowances are:
  - Calculated for a trader's period of account.
  - Deductible from adjusted trading profits.

Plant and machinery

Definition

Plant and Machinery (P&M)

'Plant' is an item **with which** the trade is carried on (active function) and not the setting **in which** it is carried on (passive function).

```
                  Function

        Active                    Passive
   Apparatus with            Setting in
   which business            which business
     carried on                carried on
```

Examples of plant and machinery

- Computers and software
- Machinery
- Cars and lorries
- Office furniture
- Movable partitions
- Air conditioning
- Alterations of buildings to install plant and machinery

Expenditure which is not 'plant and machinery'

- False ceilings (part of the building)
- Fixed partitions

Pro forma – Capital allowances computation for unincorporated businesses

	£	Main pool £	Special rate pool £	Short life asset £	Private use asset £	Allowances £
TWDV b/f		X	X	X		
Additions not qualifying for AIA or FYA:						
Second-hand zero emission cars		X				
Cars (1-50g/km)		X				
Cars (over 50g/km)			X			
Car or other asset with private use					X	
Additions qualifying for AIA:						
Special rate pool expenditure	X					
Less: AIA (Max £1,000,000 in total)	(X)					X
Transfer balance to special rate pool			X			
Plant and machinery	X					
Less: AIA (Max £1,000,000 in total)	(X)					X
Transfer balance to main pool		X				
Disposals (lower of original cost and sale proceeds)		(X)		(X)		
		X	X	X	X	X

	£	Main pool £	Special rate pool £	Short life asset £	Private use asset £	Allowances £
BA / (BC)				(X) / X		X / (X)
Small pools WDA						
WDA at 18%		(X)				X
WDA at 6%			(X)			X
WDA at 6%/18% (depending on emissions)					(X) × BU%	X
Additions qualifying for FYAs:						
New zero emission cars	X					
Less: FYA at 100%	(X)					X
	0					
TWDV c/f		X	X		X	
Total allowances						X

Vans, lorries and motorbikes are treated like plant and machinery and not like cars.

Exam focus

It is essential that you learn this capital allowances pro forma (and the different one for corporation tax, given in Chapter 10) in order to present your calculations in a structured manner.

Note that the main pool can also be referred to as the general pool.

Exam focus

Exam kit questions in this area:

Constructed response (section C) questions:

*   Richard Feast
*   Alfred and Amaia

The allowances

The Annual Investment Allowance (AIA)

- 100% allowance for £1,000,000 of expenditure incurred in each accounting period of 12 months.
- Applied pro rata for periods of account that are not 12 months.
- Available on acquisitions in the order:
  - special rate pool items
  - plant and machinery in main pool
  - short life assets
  - private use assets.
- **Not** available on cars.
- Not available in the accounting period in which trade ceases.
- Expenditure above the maximum qualifies for a WDA immediately.
- Do not have to claim all/any of the AIA if the taxpayer does not want to.
- Any unused AIA is lost.

Writing Down Allowances (WDA)

- WDA available on a reducing balance basis.
- 18% in main pool and on SLAs.
- Special rate pool WDA = 6%.
- Applied pro rata for periods of account that are not 12 months.
- WDA adjusted for assets with private use by owner of business.

First year allowances (FYA)

- 100% FYA available on:
  - new zero emission cars
    (not available on any other cars).
- Only available in the period of acquisition.
- Never time apportion FYA for short or long accounting periods.
- Do not have to claim all/any of the FYA if the taxpayer does not want to.
- If any of the FYA is not claimed:
  - the balance is added to the main pool after claiming WDA
  - it is eligible for WDA in the next period but the unclaimed FYA can not be claimed later.

Balancing adjustments

- Assets disposed of:
  - Deduct the sale proceeds from the relevant pool.
  - The amount deducted can never exceed the original cost of the asset.
  - A balancing adjustment may arise.

- A balancing charge (BC):
  - Can occur on any pool at any time.

- A balancing allowance (BA):
  - Can occur on a 'single asset' column at any time.
  - Only occurs on main pool or special rate pool when the business ceases to trade.

Summary of the CAs for cars

CO_2 emissions

• Zero emission cars:
   – Emissions 0g/km
   – New = FYA 100%
   – Second-hand = as for low emission cars

• Low emission cars:
   – Emissions 1 – 50g/km
   – Put in main pool
   – WDA 18% for 12 month period

• High emission cars:
   – Emissions > 50g/km
   – Put in special rate pool
   – WDA 6% for 12 month period

• Private use cars:
   – Separate column
   – WDA 18%/6% for 12 month period depending on emissions
   – FYA 100% on zero emission cars
   – BA or BC will arise on disposal
   – Adjust all allowances for BU%

The special rate pool

- Pool expenditure incurred on:
  - long life assets (LLA)
  - integral features of a building
  - thermal insulation of a building
  - high emission cars (CO_2 > 50g/km).
- Pool operates in the same way as the main pool.
- AIA is available on new expenditure in this pool (except high emission cars).
- AIA is best allocated against new expenditure in this pool first.
- WDA = 6% for a 12 month period, reducing balance basis.
- FYAs are never available on SR pool assets for individuals, but for companies they are (see Chapter 10).

- LLA = assets
  - with a working life ≥ 25 years, **and**
  - expenditure incurred ≥ £100,000 for a 12 month period (but not cars or P&M in a retail shop, showroom, hotel or office).
- Integral features of a building
  = expenditure incurred on:
  - electrical (including lighting) systems
  - cold water systems
  - space or water heating systems
  - external solar shading
  - powered systems of ventilation, air cooling or air purification
  - lifts, escalators and moving walkways.
- Thermal insulation of a building
  = expenditure on thermal insulation on any commercial building (exception = residential buildings in a property business).

The small pool WDA

- Applies to the main pool and special rate pool only
  - can claim on either or both pools
  - claim is optional.
- Available where the TWDV of the pool after current period disposals is ≤ £1,000 (value for a 12 month period).
- WDA = any amount up to £1,000 (12 month period) to write the pool down to £Nil.
- Adjust maximum pro rata if period of account is not 12 months.

Short life assets (SLA)

- Each short life asset has its own column.
- Short life means there is intention to sell/ scrap the asset within eight years of end of period of account (POA) acquired.

- AIA available but a SLA election will be beneficial if there is not enough AIA for all additions.
- A balancing allowance/charge will arise when the SLA is disposed of.
- Beneficial where asset with a short life is to be disposed of for less than its TWDV.
- Not available for cars.
- If the asset is not disposed of within eight years after the end of the POA in which it was acquired
  - the TWDV is transferred to the main pool.
- Election required for SLA treatment:
  - by first anniversary of 31 January following the end of the tax year in which the basis period, in which the asset was acquired, ends.

Private use assets

- Separate column for each private use asset.
- Pool is:
  - written down by the AIA/WDA in full, according to the length of the accounting period, or FYA
  - but actual allowance claimed is restricted to business use proportion.
- BC/BA on disposal is also restricted to business use proportion.
- Cannot claim SLA treatment.
- Not applicable for companies.

Business cessation

- Additions and disposals are allocated to relevant pools.
- No AIAs, WDAs or FYAs are given.
- Balancing adjustments arise on each pool and bring the TWDV down to £Nil:
  - TWDV positive = allowance given.
  - TWDV negative = charge arises.

VAT

VAT registered business

Include additions at the VAT-exclusive cost (unless unable to recover input tax, e.g. cars).

Non-VAT registered business

Include all additions at the VAT-inclusive cost.

Disposals

All disposals to be included at the VAT-exclusive proceeds amount.

Approach to computational questions for unincorporated businesses

For P&M capital allowances, adopt the following step-by-step approach:

(1) Read the information in the question and decide how many columns / pools you will require.

(2) Draft the layout and insert the TWDV b/f in each relevant column (does not apply in a new trade).

(3) Insert additions not eligible for the AIA or FYAs into the appropriate column taking care to allocate cars into the correct column according to CO_2 emissions.

(4) Insert additions eligible for the AIA in the first column, then allocate the AIA to the additions.

Remember to time apportion maximum AIA if the period of account is not 12 months.

Allocate the AIA to special rate pool additions in priority to additions of P&M in the main or other individual asset pools.

(5) Any special rate pool additions in excess of the AIA must be added to the special rate pool to increase the balance available for 6% WDA.

Any main pool expenditure in excess of the AIA should be added to the main pool to increase the balance qualifying for 18% WDA.

(6) Deal with any disposal by deducting the lower of cost and sale proceeds.

(7) Work out any balancing charge / balancing allowance for assets in individual columns.

Remember to adjust for any private use if an unincorporated business (not relevant for companies, see Chapter 10).

(8) Consider if the small pools WDA applies to the main pool and / or the special rate pool.

(9) Calculate the WDA on each of the pools at the appropriate rate (18% or 6%).

Remember to:

- time apportion if the period of account is not 12 months

- adjust for any private use if an unincorporated business (not relevant for companies).

(10) Insert any additions of new cars with zero emissions, which will get 100% FYA.

Remember the FYA is never time apportioned.

(11) Calculate the TWDV to carry forward to the next accounting period and total the allowances column.

(12) Deduct the total allowances from the tax adjusted trading profits.

Exam focus

Be aware of scenarios in the exam where the question asks for a computation of both an adjustment of profits and capital allowances.

Sometimes the information listed within the repairs and renewal 'notes to the accounts' could include items that should be classed as plant & machinery.

Remember to:

- disallow these items in your adjustment of profits as they are capital expenditure, but

- include them within your P&M capital allowance workings.

For example, a replacement printer could be included as a 'repair' in the statement of profit or loss. This should be disallowed in the adjustment of profits as it is a new capital item, but qualifies for AIA and WDA as P&M in the main pool.

Effect of accounting period length for unincorporated businesses

- The AIA and WDA are given for a 12 month period.
- If the period of account is less than 12 months:
  - scale down AIA and WDA
- If the period of account exceeds 12 months:
  - scale up AIA and WDA

Key Point

FYAs are always given in full regardless of the length of the period of account.

Structures and building allowances

- Available for a building constructed, extended or renovated on or after 6 April 2020 or 1 April 2020 for companies.
- 3% straight line allowance for a 12 month accounting period.
- Cost of land, legal and professional fees and planning permission do not qualify for SBAs.
- Residential buildings do not qualify.
- Only claimed from when building is brought into qualifying use.
- Separate SBAs for each building.
- SBAs are time apportioned for short or long periods.

On disposal

- Seller time apportions SBAs to date of disposal.
- No balancing allowance or balancing charge.
- Sale proceeds for calculation of gain = increased by SBAs claimed.
- Buyer receives remainder of SBAs at 3% based on original cost.

5

Sole traders: basis of assessment

In this chapter

- Basis of assessment.
- New businesses – opening year rules.
- Overlap profits.
- Business ceases – closing year rules.

Basis of assessment

Current year basis (CYB)

General rule:

Taxable trading income for a tax year

= the tax adjusted trading profit
  for the 12 month period of account
  ending in that tax year.

For example:

Accounts for the year ended 31 December
2022 = taxed in the tax year 2022/23.

New businesses – opening year rules

- Special rules to ensure there is an assessment for every tax year in which the business trades.

Tax year	Basis of assessment
First tax year (tax year in which trade starts)	Profits from date of commencement to following 5 April (Actual basis)
Second tax year (a) Period of account ending in the tax year is:	
(i) a 12 month period of account	That period of account (CYB)
(ii) less than 12 months long	The first twelve months of trading
(iii) more than 12 months long	Twelve months ending on the accounting date in the second tax year (i.e. the last 12 months of the long period of account)
(b) No period of account ending in the tax year	Actual profits from 6 April to 5 April
Third tax year	Twelve months ending on accounting date in the third tax year (usually CYB, but if a long period of account = the last 12 months of that long period)
Fourth year onwards	Normal CYB

Overlap profits

- Arise when profits are taxed more than once.
- Deducted from the final assessment when an individual ceases to trade.

Exam focus

Exam kit questions in this area:

Constructed response (section C) questions:

- Fang, Hong and Kang
- Robinette
- Sam, Tam and Uma

Business ceases – closing year rules

- Where an individual ceases to trade, any profits not yet taxed will be taxed in the tax year in which trading ceases.
- Penultimate tax year:
  - CYB.
- Final tax year:
  - Actual profit from the end of the basis period of the penultimate year of assessment to date of cessation.
  - Deduct any unrelieved overlap profits.

Key Point

Over the life of the business the profits taxed will equal the taxable profits earned by the business.

6

Partnerships

In this chapter

- Introduction.
- Basis of assessment.
- Trading income assessments.
- Partnership losses.
- Limited liability partnerships (LLP).

Introduction

- A partnership is an unincorporated business but is not a separate legal entity; it is a collection of individuals working in business together.
- The partnership itself is not taxed.
- Each partner is subject to income tax individually.

Basis of assessment

- The partnership accounting profit is adjusted in the same way as a sole trader.
- Capital allowances are claimed by the partnership, including those on the partners' own assets (e.g. cars).

  They are deducted from the adjusted trading profits to arrive at the tax adjusted trading profit of the partnership in the usual way.
- The partners are each taxed based on their allocated share of the partnership tax adjusted trading profits as if the partner were a sole trader (i.e. normally current year basis).

Trading income assessments

Treat like sole traders – each partner is an owner of the shared business.

Step 1	Determine the tax adjusted accounting profit/loss after capital allowances of the partnership for each accounting period.
Step 2	Allocate these profits or losses between the partners according to the **profit sharing agreement** (PSA) in the **accounting period**.
	If PSA requires a salary or interest on capital allocation:
	• treat as a share of the trading profits.
	The balance of profits or losses:
	• are shared in the profit sharing ratio (PSR).
	If a partner joins or leaves during the accounting period:
	• treat as if a change in PSR
	• time apportion profits, apply appropriate PSA to each part.
Step 3	Determine the taxable trading income assessment for the tax year or the loss reliefs available for each partner using that partner's share of the accounting profit/loss.
	Partner joins – opening year rules
	Partner leaves – closing year rules
	Other years – normal CYB basis (i.e. tax the profits of 12 months to a/c date)

Key Point

PSAs may allocate salaries and/or interest on fixed capital. These are taxed as a share of trading profits and not as salary or interest income.

They are allocated to the partners first and then any remaining balance of partnership profits is allocated according to the partnership profit sharing ratio (PSR).

Key Point

When a partner joins/leaves a partnership, the special opening/closing year rules only apply to the partner joining or leaving the partnership.

Continuing partners will continue to be taxed on the CYB.

Exam focus

Exam kit questions in this area:

Constructed response (section C) questions:

- Fang, Hong and Kang
- Daniel, Francine and Gregor
- Sam, Tam and Uma
- Poppy
- Amanda

Partnership losses

- Partnership losses are calculated and allocated between the partners in the same way as profits.
- Each partner may claim loss relief under the normal rules.
- Only partners joining the partnership are eligible for special opening years carry back relief.
- Only partners leaving the partnership are eligible for terminal loss relief.

Limited liability partnerships (LLP)

- An LLP is a special type of partnership where the amount that each partner may be required to contribute towards the partnership losses, debts and liabilities is limited by agreement.
- For TX, they are taxed in the same way as other partnerships (except that LLPs cannot use the cash basis, see Chapter 3).

Trading losses for individuals

In this chapter

- Ongoing businesses.
- Opening years relief.
- Terminal loss relief.
- Maximum deduction from total income.
- Procedure for dealing with loss questions.
- Choice of loss reliefs.

Ongoing businesses

Trading losses
- Calculated in the same way as a trading profit.
- Trading income assessment is £Nil.

Relief against total income
- Available in:
  - tax year of the loss and/or,
  - preceding tax year.

- Offset cannot be restricted to preserve PA.
- Offset is restricted if loss exceeds maximum amount (see later).
- Excess loss is automatically carried forward or can be set against chargeable gains.

Relief against chargeable gains
- Available in the same years as a claim against total income:
  - tax year of the loss, and/or
  - preceding tax year.
- Only possible after a claim against total income has been made in the tax year in which a claim against gains is required.
- Do not need to claim against total income in both years first.
- No maximum restriction (see later).

Relief against future trading profits

- Relieved against:
  - the first available
  - trading profits only
  - of the same trade.
- Loss offset cannot be restricted.

- Trading loss is treated as a current year capital loss.
- Deducted
  - after the offset of current year capital losses
  - before capital losses brought forward, and
  - before the AEA.

The exam could require you to identify all the options available before deciding how to offset the loss.

Order of offset

When there is more than one loss to offset:

- deal with the earliest loss first
- losses b/f are offset in priority to CY and PY claims
- watch out for the maximum restriction (if applicable) (see below).

Exam kit questions in this area:

Constructed response (section C) questions:

- Fang, Hong and Kang
- Michael and Sean
- Daniel, Francine and Gregor

Opening years relief

In addition to reliefs available for an ongoing business, special opening years loss relief is available.

- A loss incurred in any of the **first four tax years** of a new business can be set against:
  - total income
  - of the three tax years preceding the tax year of the loss
  - on a FIFO basis.
- One claim for one tax year covers carry back to all three years.
- Offset cannot be restricted to preserve PA.
- Maximum restriction applies as for ongoing loss relief against total income (see later).

Terminal loss relief

In addition to standard relief against total income and chargeable gains, special terminal loss relief is available.

Relief is given for the loss of the **last 12 months** of trading.

- Relief is:
  - against profits of the same trade
  - of the tax year of cessation, and
  - the three preceding tax years
  - on a LIFO basis.
- Calculation of the terminal loss:
  - (1) loss from 6 April to date of cessation
  - (2) plus proportion of loss in the preceding tax year starting 12 months prior to cessation date
  - (3) plus unrelieved overlap profits.

Exam focus

Exam kit questions in this area:

Constructed response (section C) question:

- Michael and Sean

Maximum deduction from total income

Maximum deduction from income other than trading income = **greater of**:

- £50,000, or
- 25% of adjusted total income (ATI).

Therefore restriction will be £50,000 unless ATI exceeds £200,000.

Adjusted total income (ATI):

	£
Total income	X
Less: Gross PPCs	(X)
ATI	X

Key Point

The maximum restriction may be beneficial as it could avoid wasting PAs.

Maximum deduction limit:

- applies to trading losses set against:
  - current year total income
  - earlier years if set against income other than profits of the same trade.
- does not apply to losses set against chargeable gains.

Offset against earlier years:

- set against profits from same trade first, then non-trading income
- no restriction to offset against profits from same trade
- restrict offset against non-trading income
- loss that cannot be set off = not lost
  - can claim to offset against chargeable gains, or
  - c/f as usual.

Procedure for dealing with loss questions

(1) Determine tax adjusted loss/profits after capital allowances for each period of account.

(2) Determine when loss relief is available (i.e. in which tax years)

 - Different options if in opening/ ongoing/ closing years.

(3) Lay out IT computations for tax years side by side

 - Leave spaces to insert losses offset.

(4) Set up a loss working for each loss to show how it is utilised.

(5) If more than one loss

 - Consider in chronological order.

(6) Consider options available depending on whether early years of business, last year of business, chargeable gains in tax year.

(7) Offset losses in most beneficial way or as instructed by the question requirement

 - Watch out for maximum restriction rules.

Choice of loss reliefs

- To choose the most appropriate claim:
  - obtain relief at the highest marginal tax rate
  - obtain relief as early as possible
  - avoid wasting PAs (and the AEA for CGT where appropriate).
- Relief against total income and special opening year relief give earliest relief, rather than carry forward loss relief.
- A large gain in a single year (the year of loss or year immediately preceding):
  - indicates that a claim against chargeable gains may be beneficial
  - but must relieve total income of same year first and maximum restriction may apply
  - may result in wastage of PAs
  - maximum restriction does not apply against gains
- relief against gains is at 10% or 20% depending on the taxpayer's remaining basic rate band (18% or 28% if the gain resulted from the disposal of residential property).
- Relief against total income and special opening years relief are optional but carrying forward the loss is mandatory and automatic if no specific claim is made.
- No partial claims allowed (i.e. all or nothing reliefs).
- Relief against total income applies to two years but separate claims are required for each year and such claims can be made in either order.
- The best claim may be a compromise of the main objectives (e.g. may accept lower tax saving if relief is given earlier).

8

Pensions and national insurance

In this chapter

- Pension contributions.
- National insurance contributions (NICs).
- Employees.
- Employers.
- Self-employed individuals.

Pension contributions

Types of pension scheme:

- Occupational pension schemes (set up by employers for their employees)
- Personal pension schemes (available to any individual).

Exam focus

Exam kit questions in this area:

OT case (section B) question:

- Philip and Charles

Constructed response (section C) questions:

- Patience
- Richard Tryer
- John Beach
- Dembe
- Kioni

Tax relief for pension contributions:

- Any amount can be contributed by an individual into any number of pension schemes, but **tax relief** is only available on a **maximum amount** each year.

- Tax relief available on contributions up to the **lower** of:

  (a) Total gross contributions paid

  (b) Maximum amount = higher of:

    (i) £3,600 and

    (ii) 100% x (relevant earnings).

- Relevant earnings:

  - trading profits

  - employment income

  - furnished holiday letting income.

- An individual with no relevant earnings can therefore obtain tax relief on contributions of up to £3,600 per year.

Method of giving tax relief

Employee contributions

> Pension contribution to:

- Personal pension scheme
  - Basic rate relief (20%) given at source.
  - Higher rate relief given by extending basic rate band.
  - Additional rate relief given by extending higher rate band.

- Occupational scheme
  - Tax relief at all rates given at source through PAYE system (i.e. an allowable deduction against employment income).

Employer contributions

- Not treated as a taxable benefit.
- Tax deductible for employer.
- Taken into account when calculating total contributions to be compared with annual allowance (AA).

Annual Allowance (AA)

- Where total contributions paid into pension schemes > the current year AA plus unused AA b/f:
  - a tax charge arises on the excess.
- The tax charge is:
  - taxed as the individual's top slice of income
  - paid through the self-assessment system.

Exam focus

In the examination:

- add the excess to the taxpayer's total income, and
- tax that part last (i.e. after dividends).

- Unused AA b/f from the **previous three tax years** is taken into account:
  - can only be c/f if the individual was a member of a pension scheme for that tax year.
- The AA for the three years prior to 2022/23 was £40,000
- Order of utilisation:
  - current year AA is used first
  - then earlier three years unused amount, on a FIFO basis.

Restriction of annual allowance – high income individuals

- The annual allowance is gradually reduced for individuals with high income.
- The restriction applies to individuals with 'adjusted income' exceeding £240,000.
- The annual allowance is reduced by: (Adjusted income – £240,000) × 50%.

- The maximum reduction to the annual allowance is £36,000, which means the minimum annual allowance will be £4,000.

Adjusted income	£
Net income (from the income tax computation)	x
Plus: Individual **employee's occupational pension** contributions	x
Employer's contributions into any scheme for that individual	x
Adjusted income	x

Accessing the pension fund

- Minimum age for accessing pension fund is 55.
  - Can withdraw 25% of the fund as a tax-free lump sum.
  - Balance (remaining 75%) of the fund, can be accessed in a variety of ways.
  - Withdrawals from the balance of the fund are taxed as non-savings income in the tax year they are withdrawn at the normal rates of tax (i.e. 20%, 40% or 45%).

Lifetime Allowance (LA)

- LA = Total pension value that can obtain tax relief.
- LA for 2022/23 is £1,073,100.
- Considered when an individual becomes entitled to take benefits out of the pension scheme
  (e.g. the individual becomes entitled to a pension).
- If the value of the pension fund at that time exceeds the LA; an additional tax charge arises.
- Calculation of this tax charge is not examinable.

National insurance contributions (NICs)

- Different classes of NICs are paid depending on the individual's status.

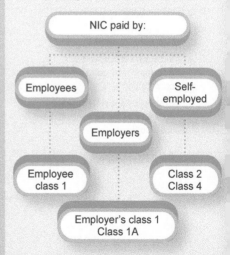

Employees

Employee class 1

- Employees pay class 1 NICs on their 'cash earnings'.
- Cash earnings includes:
  - any remuneration derived from employment and paid in money
  - vouchers exchangeable for cash or goods
  - reimbursement of cost of travel between home and work.
- Cash earnings does not include:
  - exempt employment benefits
  - most non-cash benefits
  - reimbursement of business expenses
  - mileage allowance up to 45p per mile.
- Payable by all employees aged 16 to state pension age.

- Payable at 13.25% on earnings between £12,570 and £50,270.
- Payable at 3.25% on earnings above £50,270.
- Contributions are collected by the employer through the PAYE scheme.

Exam focus

Exam kit questions in this area:

Constructed response (section C) questions:

- George
- Sophia Wong
- John Beach
- Richard Feast
- Kioni
- Jade

Employers

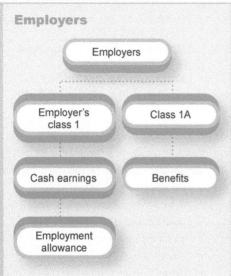

Employer's class 1

- Cost borne by employer.
- Allowable trading expense for tax purposes.
- Rate of 15.05% on earnings over £9,100 per annum.
  - Note: no upper limit.
- Paid on 'cash earnings', as for employee class 1.
- Paid in respect of employees aged ≥ 16.
  - Note: no upper limit.
- Employment allowance available.
- Payable with employee class 1 contributions through PAYE system.
- Payable on 22nd of the next month (electronic payments), or 19th of the next month if not paid electronically.

 Exam focus

The electronic payday should be quoted in the examination as most businesses pay electronically.

Employment allowance

- Up to £5,000 p.a. allowance.
- Deducted from employer's class 1 NICs only.
- Claimed though the PAYE system.
- Employment allowance not available to:
  - Companies where a director is the sole employee paid above £9,100.
  - Employers with total class 1 employer's NIC ≥ £100,000 in previous tax year.

Class 1A

- Payable by the employer only.
- Rate of 15.05% on taxable benefits provided to the employee.
- Payable by 22 July following the tax year (if paid electronically) or 19 July (if not paid electronically).

Exam focus

Exam kit questions in this area:
Constructed response (section C) questions:

- Richard Feast
- John Beach
- Kioni

Self-employed individuals

Self-employed

Class 2
- Fixed at £3.15 per week.
- Paid at the same time as the balancing payment for income tax under self-assessment.

Class 4
- Paid on taxable trade profits less losses b/f.
- Rate of 10.25% on profits which fall between £12,570 and £50,270.
- Rate of 3.25% on profits which exceed £50,270.
- Paid at the same time as income tax under self-assessment.
- Not payable if over state pension age or under 16 at the **start** of the tax year.

Key Point

Self-employed individuals who have employees pay:

- Class 2 and class 4 NICs in respect of their unincorporated trade, and
- Employer's class 1 and class 1A NICs in respect of earnings and benefits provided to employees.

Exam focus

Exam kit questions in this area:
Constructed response (section C) questions

- Carol Courier
- George
- Dembe

9

Ethics and tax administration for individuals

In this chapter

- Professional Code of Ethics.
- Self-assessment.
- Records.
- Payment of income tax and class 4 NICs.
- Payment of class 2 NICs.
- Payment of capital gains tax.
- Interest.
- Claims.
- Penalties.
- HMRC compliance checks.
- Discovery assessments.
- Appeals.
- PAYE.

Professional Code of Ethics

Principles

- Objectivity
- Professional behaviour
- Professional competence and due care
- Integrity
- Confidentiality.

Key Point

Remember: OPPIC.

Tax evasion versus tax avoidance

- Tax evasion
  - unlawful
  - e.g. suppressing information or submitting false information
  - client = subject to criminal prosecution / fines / imprisonment
  - adviser = subject to sanctions of criminal law.

- Tax avoidance
  - use of the taxation system to legitimately reduce tax
  - e.g. advice to reduce tax liability
  - also used to describe tax schemes devised to utilise loopholes in the tax legislation.

- Specific tax avoidance schemes have been targeted with anti-avoidance legislation.

- HMRC have also introduced:
  - Disclosure obligations re specific tax avoidance schemes.
  - A general anti-abuse rule (GAAR) to counter artificial and abusive schemes to avoid tax. This targets arrangements which cannot be regarded as a reasonable course of action.

Dealing with HMRC

- Information provided must be accurate and complete.
- Must not assist a client to plan or commit an offence.
- If become aware of a tax irregularity:
  - discuss with client
  - ensure proper disclosure to HMRC.

- Client error
  - decide whether genuine or deliberate / fraudulent act
  - explain to client the need to notify HMRC
  - prompt / adequate disclosure taken into account when deciding penalties
  - if client refuses
    - must explain potential consequences in writing
    - if material, consider whether to continue to act for client
  - if client still refuses
    - should cease to act and write to HMRC stating that the firm no longer acts for the client but not stating the reason why.

Money laundering regulations

Definition

Money laundering = benefiting from or concealing the proceeds of crime

- includes the proceeds of tax evasion.

A member of ACCA must appoint a Money Laundering Reporting Officer (MLRO):

- MLRO decides whether to report a transaction to the National Crime Agency (NCA)
- if a report is made, client should not be informed as this is an offence (known as 'tipping off').

Dishonest conduct of tax agents

- Incurs a civil penalty of up to £50,000.
- HMRC may:
  - publish penalised tax agent's details
  - access working papers of a dishonest agent.

Self-assessment

Filing for returns

- Later of:
  - 31 October 2023 (paper return).
  - 31 January 2024 (electronic return).
  - Three months after the issue of the notice to file a return.
- Fixed and tax-geared penalties may apply for late filing (see later).

Notification of chargeability

- Must notify HMRC of income or chargeable gains on which tax is due:
  - within six months from the end of the tax year in which the liability arises
  - i.e. by 5 October 2023 for 2022/23.
- standard penalty may arise for failure to notify chargeability (see later).

Exam focus

Exam kit questions in this area:
Constructed response (section C) question:

- Richard Feast

Amendments to the return

- HMRC can amend return < 9 months of the actual filing date.
- Taxpayer can amend < 12 months of the 31 January filing date.

Determination of tax

- Issued by HMRC when a return is not filed by the 31 January filing date.
- Can be issued by HMRC within three years from the filing date (i.e. by 31 January 2027 for 2022/23 tax return).
- Assessment = replaced by the actual self-assessment return when it is submitted.

Exam focus

All of the topics in this chapter (ethics and tax administration) could be tested easily as objective test questions in the TX examination.

Exam kit questions in this area:

Constructed response (section C) question

- Richard Feast
- Harbour Ltd
- Jade

Records

Business records

- A business must keep records of:
  - all receipts and expenses
  - all goods purchased and sold
  - all supporting documents relating to the transactions of the business, such as accounts, books, contracts, vouchers.
- Self-employed taxpayers must retain all their records (not just business records) for five years after the 31 January following the end of the tax year.

  For 2022/23 = until 31 January 2029.

Other records

- Other taxpayers should keep evidence of income received.
- Must normally be retained for 12 months after the 31 January following the end of the tax year.

  For 2022/23 = until 31 January 2025.

Penalty

- A fixed penalty of up to £3,000 may be charged for failure to keep or retain adequate records.

Payment of income tax and class 4 NICs

Income tax and class 4 NICs are due as follows:

- Two equal payments on account (POA):
  - 31 January in the tax year (31.1.2023 for 2022/23)
  - 31 July after tax year (31.7.2023 for 2022/23).
- Balancing payment due:
  - 31 January after the tax year (31.1.2024 for 2022/23).
- Each POA is 50% of the previous year's income tax and class 4 NICs liability after the deduction of PAYE (= the relevant amount).
- POAs are not required if:
  - the relevant amount for the previous year is < £1,000, or
  - more than 80% of the income tax liability for the previous year was met by deduction of tax at source i.e. PAYE.

Exam focus

Exam kit questions in this area:

Constructed response (section C) questions:

- Sophie Shape
- George

Claims to reduce POAs

- At any time before 31 January following the tax year, a taxpayer can claim to reduce the POAs.

- Should only claim to reduce POAs if the tax liability (net of PAYE) for the current year is expected to be less than the POAs, based on the previous year's tax liability.

- An incorrect claim can lead to interest and penalties.

Exam focus

Exam kit questions in this area:

Constructed response (section C) questions:

- Sophie Shape

- Zhi

Payment of class 2 NICs

Class 2 NICs are payable under the self-assessment system and are due by:

- 31 January after the tax year (31.1.2024 for 2022/23)

- POAs are not made for class 2 NIC.

Payment of capital gains tax

- Disposals of UK residential property are reported to HMRC within 60 days of completion and the relevant CGT liability paid at the same time.

- Rate of CGT depends on the estimated amount of taxpayer's taxable income at the time of disposal.

Interest

Late payment interest

Charged on:

- all late payments of tax
- at a daily rate
- runs from: due date
- to: date of payment.

Exam focus

All calculations in the examination will be to the nearest month unless the question states otherwise.

Repayment interest

HMRC pay interest on any overpaid tax

- from: later of
  - date tax due, or
  - date HMRC received tax
- to: date of repayment.

Interest on excessive claims to reduce POAs

- The interest charge is based on the difference between:
    - the amount actually paid, and
    - the amount that should have been paid.
- The amount that should have been paid = the lower of:
    - the original POAs based on the relevant amount for the previous year, and
    - 50% of the final tax liability (net of tax deducted at source) for the current year.
- Interest runs:
    - from: the due dates of
        31 January in the tax year and
        31 July following the tax year
    - to: the date of payment.

Claims

- Claims are usually made in the self-assessment return and must be quantified at the time of the claim.
- A claim which affects an earlier year (e.g. loss carry back), does not amend the earlier year but the tax saving is calculated as if the earlier year is amended.
- Carry back claims do not therefore reduce POAs for the year following the earlier year.
- The taxpayer can make a claim for overpayment relief to reduce tax within four years following the tax year concerned. A claim can be made in respect of errors made and mistakes arising from not understanding the law.

Penalties

Standard penalties

Applies in two circumstances:

- Submission of incorrect returns:
  - All taxes.
- Failure to notify liability to tax:
  - Income tax, CGT, corporation tax, VAT and NIC.
- Penalty = % of potential lost revenue.
- Depends on the behaviour of the taxpayer.

Taxpayer behaviour	Maximum penalty (% of revenue lost)	Minimum penalty - unprompted disclosure	Minimum penalty - prompted disclosure
Genuine mistake (for incorrect returns only)	No penalty		
Careless / Failure to take reasonable care	30%	0%	15%
Deliberate but no concealment	70%	20%	35%
Deliberate with concealment	100%	30%	50%

- Penalties may be reduced at HMRC discretion where the taxpayer informs HMRC
  - larger reductions for unprompted disclosure.
- An unprompted disclosure = where the taxpayer informs HMRC when they had no reason to believe HMRC have noticed, or are about to discover the error.
- Taxpayer can appeal against a standard penalty.

Other penalties relating to individuals

Offence	Penalty
Late filing of self-assessment tax return	
– filed after due date	£100 fixed penalty
Additional penalties:	
– filed 3 months late	Daily penalties of £10 per day (maximum of 90 days) in addition to £100 fixed penalty
– filed 6 months late	5% of tax due (minimum £300) plus above penalties
– more than 12 months after filing date where withholding information was:	The penalties above plus:
– not deliberate	Additional 5% of tax due (minimum £300)
– deliberate but no concealment	70% of tax due (minimum £300)
– deliberate with concealment	100% of tax due (minimum £300)

Offence	Penalty
Late payment of tax – Paid > 1 month late – Paid > 6 months late – Paid > 12 months late	 5% of tax due Additional 5% Additional 5% Applies to balancing payments only (not POAs).

Fraud or negligence on claiming reduced POAs	£
	POAs if claim not made X
	Less: POAs actually paid (X)
	       ――
	       X

Failure to keep and retain required records	Up to £3,000 per tax year

Note that 'tax' for an individual will include income tax, capital gains tax and NIC.

Exam focus

Exam kit questions in this area:

Constructed response (section C) questions:

- Poppy

HMRC compliance checks

- HMRC has the right to enquire into the completeness and accuracy of any return.
- Must issue written notice before commencing a compliance check (enquiry)
  - within 12 months of the date the return is actually filed.
- On completion of a compliance check, HMRC must send the taxpayer a completion notice:
  - either stating no amendment required, or
  - amending the taxpayer's self-assessment.
- Taxpayer has 30 days to appeal against HMRC's amendment.

Exam focus

Exam kit questions in this area:

Constructed response (section C) questions:

- Richard Feast
- Sophie Shape
- Robinette

Discovery assessments

- HMRC can raise a discovery assessment if they discover an inaccuracy in the return within:

	Time from end of tax year	For 2022/23
Basic time limit	Four years	5 April 2027
Careless error	Six years	5 April 2029
Deliberate error	Twenty years	5 April 2043

Appeals

Appeals to resolve disputes with HMRC

- Taxpayer can appeal against a decision made by HMRC
    - in writing
    - within 30 days of the disputed decision.
- They can proceed in one of two ways:
    - request a review by another HMRC officer, or
    - refer case to an independent Tax Tribunal.

Tax Tribunals

Two tiers (layers) of Tax Tribunal system:

- First-tier Tribunal, and
- Upper Tribunal.

The First-tier Tribunal deals with:

- Default paper cases:
    - simple appeals (e.g. against a fixed penalty)
    - usually no hearing provided both sides agree.
- Basic cases:
    - straightforward appeals
    - minimal exchange of paperwork
    - a short hearing.
- Standard cases:
    - more detailed consideration of issues
    - more formal hearing.

- Complex cases:
  - may be heard by the First-tier
  - however usually heard by Upper Tribunal.

The Upper Tribunal will deal with:

- Complex cases
  - requiring detailed specialist knowledge
  - a formal hearing.

Hearings are held in public and decisions are published.

A decision of the Upper Tribunal:

- may be appealed to the Court of Appeal
- but only on grounds of a point of law.

PAYE

- Under PAYE an employee's employment income tax liability is deducted from the employee's remuneration and paid to HMRC by the employer.
- Each employee is given a code number to ensure that the tax collected at each pay date is the correct proportion of the tax due for the whole year.
- The code number is calculated from allowances and deductions.
- Allowances:
  - personal allowances
  - allowable interest paid
  - expenses deductible from earnings.

- Deductions:
  - benefits - but not if they were 'payrolled' i.e. taxed under PAYE
  - any untaxed income on which the tax liability is discharged by set-off against allowances
  - any adjustment to cover tax underpaid in previous years (provided underpaid tax < £3,000).
- The code is 1/10th of net allowances rounded down to the nearest whole number.

Administration / forms

- Employers with less than 250 employees may make their monthly PAYE payments by cheque or electronically.
- Employers with 250 or more employees must pay electronically.
- PAYE/NIC payable to HMRC on 22nd of every month (electronic payment), on 19th if payments made by cheque.
- Employers with average monthly PAYE and NIC payments of less than £1,500:
  - can make quarterly payments
  - by 22nd of month following 5 July, 5 October, 5 January, 5 April (electronic payment).

Exam focus

As most employers now pay electronically, the pay day of 22nd of every month should be used in the examination.

Real time information (RTI)

- Employers must submit PAYE / NIC information to HMRC electronically when or before employees are paid each week or month.

- A year end summary = provided with the final RTI submission for the tax year.

- HMRC will charge penalties for late submissions of RTI:

  - no penalty is imposed for the first month that a late payment is made

  - a penalty of £100-£400 is applied for subsequent late payments. The amount depends on the number of employees.

- An additional penalty of 5% of the PAYE/NIC due can be imposed once a payment is three months late.

Key forms

- P45 – when employee leaves.

- P60 – end of year summary
  – provided to employee by 31 May.

- P11D – summary of benefits
  – provided to employee by 6 July.

Exam focus

Exam kit questions in this area:

Constructed response (section C) question:

- Long Ltd and Road Ltd

10

Corporation tax

In this chapter

- Principles of corporation tax.
- Accounting periods.
- Pro forma – corporation tax.
- Trading income.
- Company capital allowances.
- Property income.
- Interest.
- Qualifying charitable donations.
- Long period of account.

Exam focus

Corporation tax is an important topic area of the syllabus.

It will be the focus of a 15 mark question in section C.

It is also very likely to be tested in both sections A and B.

Principles of corporation tax

Companies **resident** in the UK pay corporation tax on their **worldwide** profits (including chargeable gains but excluding dividends).

Definition

A company is resident in the UK if it is:

* incorporated in the UK, or
* it is an overseas company and its central management and control is exercised in the UK.

Companies pay corporation tax on their taxable total profits (TTP) for an accounting period (AP).

Exam focus

Exam kit questions in this area:

Constructed response (section C) questions:

* Lena Ltd, Mekong Ltd & Nile Ltd

Accounting periods (APs)

- An AP is usually the company's period of account (i.e. the period for which the company prepares its accounts).
- An AP cannot exceed 12 months.
- If a period of account exceeds 12 months, the period is split into two APs (see later).

Key Point

An AP can be any length up to 12 months but can never exceed 12 months.

Pro forma – corporation tax

Corporation tax computation for the accounting period of…months ended…

	Notes	£
Trading profit	(1)	X
Property income		X
Interest income	(2)	X
Chargeable gains	(3)	X
Total profits		X
Less: Loss relief – CY, C/B		(X)
Less: Loss relief b/f		(X)
Less: QCD relief	(4)	(X)
		X
Less: Group relief		(X)
Taxable total profits (TTP)		X
Corporation tax: TTP x 19% (5)		X

It is essential to learn and use this pro forma.

Notes

(1) Tax adjusted trading profit less capital allowances.

(2) Net interest income on non-trade loan relationships.

(3) Chargeable gains net of current year and brought forward capital losses.

(4) Qualifying charitable donations (QCDs) = all charitable donations by a company (except those allowed as a trading expense) (see later).

(5) The rate of corporation tax is fixed for each financial year. The rate for FY2022 is 19%.

Dividends received from UK companies are exempt, and therefore are:

- not included in TTP, and

- not subject to corporation tax.

When calculating the TTP:

(i) Start your answer by laying out the CT pro forma, listing all income types and deducting QCDs.

(ii) Prepare separate workings for each element of the computation. Insert the relevant figures in the pro forma and cross-reference the figures clearly.

Exam kit questions in this area:

Constructed response (section C) questions:

- Harbour Ltd
- Maison Ltd
- E-commerce plc
- Lucky Ltd
- Clueless Ltd
- Long Ltd and Road Ltd
- Mooncake Ltd

Trading income

A company's trading profit is adjusted for tax purposes.

Adjustment to profits and capital allowances for companies

Computed in the same way as for individuals (Chapters 3 and 4) except for:

- no private use adjustments
- interest payable/receivable
  - loan relationship rules apply
- capital allowances
  - no private use assets
  - where period of account > 12 months, separate capital allowance computations required for each AP
  - From 1 April 2021, companies have two extra types of first year allowance, not available to unincorporated businesses. Details of these are below.

Company capital allowances

Enhanced capital allowances

Companies purchasing new plant and machinery between 1 April 2021 and 31 March 2023 will be eligible to claim:

- **130% super deduction** for main pool assets

- **50% first year allowance (FYA)** for special rate pool assets.

The new reliefs are not available on:

- Second-hand assets (but these can still get AIA, except for cars)

- Cars

- Assets bought in the final period of trading.

130% super deduction should be claimed **instead of AIA**. These assets should be kept in a separate FYA column.

Special rate pool expenditure

For new special rate pool additions (other than cars) follow these steps:

1. Claim **AIA first** (gives 100% relief) as far as possible

2. Claim **50% FYA** on remaining cost

3. Transfer remaining expenditure, after deducting FYA, to the special rate pool (only gets 6% WDA from **following AP**).

Questions will not be set involving the disposal of an asset on which enhanced capital allowances were claimed or where enhanced capital allowance expenditure is incurred in a period spanning 31 March 2023.

Effect of accounting period length for companies

The AIA and WDA are given for a 12 month period.

- If the period of account is less than 12 months:
  - AIA and WDA will be scaled down
  - FYAs are always given in full.
- If the period of account is more than 12 months:
  - split period into two accounting periods (AP) because an AP cannot exceed 12 months for a company
  - remember that the second AP will be less than 12 months; therefore the AIA and WDA will be scaled down in that AP.

FYAs are always given in full regardless of the length of the period of account.

Exam kit questions on this area:

OT case (section B) question:

- Greenzone Ltd

Constructed response (section C) questions:

- Aoede Ltd, Bianca Ltd and Charon Ltd
- Lucky Ltd
- Retro Ltd
- Clueless Ltd
- Lena Ltd, Mekong Ltd & Nile Ltd
- Jump Ltd
- E-Commerce Ltd
- Long Ltd and Road Ltd
- Mixture Ltd

Capital allowances pro forma for companies

	AIA	FYA	Main pool	SRP	SLA	Allowances
Year ended	£	£	£	£	£	£
TWDV b/f			X	X	X	
Additions: No AIA (Cars)			X	X		
Additions: With super deduction (X × 130%)		X				
Super deduction @ 130%		(X)				X
		___				
		0				
Additions: With AIA						
SRP additions (pre 1.4.21)	X					
AIA (Max £1,000,000 in total)	(X)					X
	___					
				X		
MP additions (second-hand/pre 1.4.21)	X					
AIA (Max £1,000,000 in total)	(X)					X
	___					
			X			
SRP additions (on/after 1.4.21)	X					
AIA (Max £1,000,000 in total)	(X)					X
	___					
Balance of SRP expenditure for FYA		X				

	AIA	FYA	Main pool	SRP	SLA	Allowances
Disposals			(X)		(X)	
			X	X	X	
BA/BC					(X)/X	X/(X)
Small pool WDA						
WDA @ 18%			(X)			X
WDA @ 6%				(X)		X
Additions: With FYA						
Enhanced FYA @ 50% on balance of SRP expenditure		(X)				X
		‾‾‾		X		
Zero emission cars		X				
FYA @ 100%		(X)				X
		‾‾‾	0			
TWDV c/f			X	X		
Total allowances						X

Property income

The rules for calculating property income are the same as for individuals (Chapter 1) except as follows:

- company is taxed on the profit arising in the AP (not the tax year)
- companies are always taxed on an accruals basis
- interest payable on a loan to acquire investment property is deducted from interest income (not the IT liability/property income as for an individual)
- no rent-a-room relief
- treatment of property losses (see below).

Property losses

- Property income and losses on different properties are pooled.
- If there is a net loss in one AP:
  - set first against total profits (before QCDs) of the same AP automatically
  - any excess loss is carried forward and a claim can be made to offset it against total profits (before QCDs) in future. Partial claims are allowed.

Exam focus

Exam kit questions in this area:

Constructed response (section C) questions:

- Maison Ltd
- E-commerce plc
- Harbour Ltd
- Mooncake Ltd
- Mixture Ltd

Interest

Interest income

- Taxed according to the loan relationship rules.

- In the TX examination all interest is received gross by a company.

- All interest receivable and payable on loans used for non-trading purposes is taxed as interest income.

- Incidental costs of raising loan finance such as arrangement fees and loans written off are also dealt with under these rules.

- In the exam – assume that all interest receivable is for non-trade purposes (e.g. interest receivable on bank/building society accounts).

- Deduct interest receivable in adjustment to profits computation.

- Include in CT computation as interest income.

- Tax on the accruals basis.

Exam focus

Exam kit questions in this area:

Constructed response (section C) questions:

- E-commerce plc
- Lucky Ltd
- Clueless Ltd
- Long Ltd and Road Ltd
- Fogo Ltd and Netta Ltd

Interest payable

Interest payable

Non-trade loans

Trade loans

Deducted from Interest Income

Deducted from trading profits

e.g. loan to purchase investment property or shares in another company

e.g. bank overdraft interest, loan to acquire plant, machinery, factory

- Interest paid is deductible on the accruals basis.

- **Qualifying charitable donations (QCDs)**
- Relief is available for all charitable donations made by a company:
  - Small donations to local charities = allowable trading expense
  - other charitable donations = allowable deductions from total profits, known as QCD relief.
- The amount **paid** in the AP is deducted from total profits.
- All charitable donations by companies = paid gross.
- If QCD relief exceeds total profits:
  - no relief available for the excess (unless part of a group) (see Chapter 12).

Long period of account

Accounting period > 12 months must be split into two APs:

- First 12 months
- Remainder.

For each AP, HMRC require:

- a separate CT comp, and
- a separate CT return.

Note there will be:

- Two separate pay days if a non-large company (i.e. nine months and one day after end of each AP)
- But only one file date for the returns (i.e. 12 months after end of long period of account).

Splitting the profits:

Tax adjusted trading profit before CAs	Time apportion
Capital allowances	Separate computations (where the AP is less than 12 months, the WDA/AIA is reduced accordingly, but not FYA)
Interest/Property/Other income	Calculate accrued amount for each period separately (Note)
Chargeable gains	According to date of disposal
Qualifying charitable donations	According to date paid

Note: if information to apply the strict accruals basis is not available; time apportion.

11

Losses for companies

In this chapter

- Trading losses.
- Carry back relief.
- Choice of loss relief.
- Pro forma – trading loss.
- Capital losses.
- Property losses.

Trading losses

- Trading losses for tax purposes are computed in the same way as tax adjusted trading profits.
- Where there is a loss the trading income assessment is £Nil.

The trading loss can be relieved as follows:

- Current year relief.
- Carry back relief.
- Carry forward.

Exam focus

Order of offset

When there is more than one loss to offset:

- deal with the earliest loss first.

Summary of reliefs

Carry forward relief	Current year relief	Carry back relief
		Current year offset first then carry back 12 months

• Offset against:
  – Total profits (income and gains)
  – Before QCD relief
• Optional claim
• Partial claim possible
• Indefinite carry forward
	• Offset against
	  – Total profits (income and gains)
	  – Before QCD relief
	• Carry forward any remaining losses
	• Must offset maximum amount possible if claimed
	• QCD relief is lost if no profits to offset against
	• Optional claim	

Carry back relief

- Can only be made if there are losses remaining after a current year claim.
- Carry back against total profits before QCD relief of the 12 months preceding the loss-making period
  - usually = previous set of accounts
  - if previous accounts < 12 months:
    (1) carry back 12 months on a LIFO basis, and
    (2) time apportion profits of earliest accounts.
- Where loss-making period is less than 12 months
  - no apportionment is necessary
  - carry back against profits arising in previous 12 months.

- Where a company ceases to trade the loss during the final 12 months of trading:
  - can be carried back, after a current period claim, and
  - offset against the total profits before QCD relief of the preceding 36 months
  - on a LIFO basis.

Exam focus

Exam kit questions in this area:
Constructed response (section C) questions:

- Retro Ltd
- Long Ltd and Road Ltd
- Jump Ltd
- Last Orders Ltd
- Aoede Ltd, Bianca Ltd and Charon Ltd
- Mooncake Ltd

Choice of loss relief

Factors influencing choice of loss relief

Tax saving:

- Aim is to save tax at the highest possible rate.
- As the tax rate hasn't changed for a number of years, the tax saving will be the same regardless, unless QCDs are wasted (see below).

Cash flow:

- A carry back claim may result in a repayment of tax.
- A carry forward claim will only result in a reduction of future tax.

Qualifying charitable donations:

- Unrelieved QCDs cannot be carried forward.
- Loss relief claims may result in the relief for QCDs being lost.

Pro forma – trading loss

	2021	2022	2023
	£	£	£
Trading profit	X	0	X
Other income	X	X	X
Net chargeable gains	X	X	X
Total profits	X	X	X
Less: Loss relief			
– Current year		(X)1	
– Carry back	(X)2		
	0	0	X
Less: Loss b/f		–	(X)3
Less: QCD relief	Wasted	Wasted	(X)
Taxable total profits	0	0	X

Key Point

2022 is the loss-making year. The trading profit assessment in this year is £Nil.

Keep a separate working for the loss, showing how it is utilised.

Assuming there is sufficient loss available, and assuming that the loss is being relieved as early as possible, the order in which to off-set the loss is as follows:

(1) Current year relief; in the year the loss is made.

(2) Prior year relief; carrying available losses back 12 months.

(3) Carry forward relief.

Exam focus

Use the loss pro forma to help you adopt a methodical approach to a question involving trading losses.

Approach to loss offset

(1) Lay out years – columnar form.

(2) Calculate TTP ignoring losses.

(3) Choose loss relief by reference to:
- cash flow
  - carry back may result in a repayment of tax
  - carry forward will only result in a reduction of future tax
- offset as soon as possible
- wastage of QCD relief
  - unrelieved amounts cannot be carried forward.

(4) Use separate loss working.

(5) If more than one loss, deal with earliest first and do a working for each loss.

Capital losses

- Automatically relieved against current year gains.
- Any excess losses are carried forward and relieved against first available future gains.

Key Point

Capital losses:
- cannot be carried back
- can only be relieved against gains (i.e. not other income).

Property losses

- Property losses are utilised:
  - against total profits, before QCD relief, of the current period
  - any excess losses can be carried forward against total profits, before QCD relief, of future periods.
- Losses can only be carried forward if the property business is still being carried on.
- Current period relief is mandatory.
- A claim is required for carry forward relief.
- Partial relief is allowed if a carry forward claim is made. This is not possible where the loss is relieved in the current year.
- Property losses are offset before trading losses.

Key Point

Property losses cannot be carried back.

12

Groups of companies

In this chapter

- Group relief.
- Capital gains groups.

- When tackling a group question you will need to interpret the group structure from a tax point of view.

  It is important to identify the various groups involved and the reliefs available.

- When revising groups you must learn the definition of a group for each relief and the direction of the relief.

Group relief

- Group loss relief is available to the UK members of a 75% group.
- A group relief group includes the parent company and its 75% subsidiaries.
- Parent company must:
  - have 75% of share capital, and
  - be entitled to 75% of the profits and assets on a winding up.
- Includes indirect holdings, but the parent must have an effective 75% interest in the subsidiary.
- The rules allow group relief groups to be established through companies resident anywhere in the world.
- However, in the TX examination, loss relief can only be claimed by companies that are resident in the UK.

Reliefs that are available to members of a 75% group relief group

- Any UK company in the group can surrender its loss:
  - to any other UK company in the group
  - in any direction.

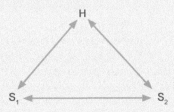

KAPLAN PUBLISHING

149

Surrendering company rules

- Losses which may be surrendered are:
  - **trading losses**
    - current period
    - brought forward trading losses to the extent that they cannot be used against the surrendering company's own total profits
  - **unrelieved** QCDs
  - **unrelieved** property business losses
    - current period and brought forward losses.
- QCDs and property losses are 'unrelieved' if they exceed any other income and gains **before** the deduction of any losses.
- Capital losses cannot be group relieved, however a separate relief is available under the capital gains group rules (see later).

Claimant company rules

- The claimant company can only accept losses that it can utilise in the current period:

	£
Total profits	X
Less: Losses b/f (full amount)	(X)
Less: Current year losses	(X)
Less: QCD relief	(X)
Maximum loss claim	X

  Note: The company's own losses (if any) are taken into account in computing the maximum group relief claim available. However, relief for the company's own losses need not be actually claimed.

- Group relief is deducted from the claimant company's TTP (i.e. after QCD relief).

Non-coterminous accounting periods

- Group relief can be claimed in the corresponding accounting period (CP).
- The CP is the period common to the accounting periods of both the surrendering company and claimant company.
- Profits and losses must be time-apportioned if:
  - the accounting periods are non-coterminous, or
  - one company has joined or left the group part way through the period.
- The surrendering company can only surrender the time-apportioned loss of the CP.
- The claimant company can only relieve against time-apportioned TTP for the CP.

- The maximum group relief is therefore the lower of:
  - the loss of the CP, and
  - the TTP of the claimant company of the CP.

Exam focus

Exam kit questions in this area:

OT case (section B) question:

- Deutsch Ltd

Constructed response (section C) questions:

- Long Ltd and Road Ltd
- Jump Ltd

Due date for group relief claim

- 12 months after the claimant company's filing date for the AP covered by the claim (i.e. usually 2 years after the end of the AP).

Payment for group relief

- The claimant company may pay the surrendering company for the loss.

- Any such payment for the group relief is ignored in both companies' CT computations.

Tax loss planning

- Consider:
  - whether to surrender
  - order of surrender.

- Group relief rules are more flexible than rules for using own loss (i.e. can specify amount to be surrendered).

- Can restrict amount of group relief loss surrender, to retain sufficient loss to preserve QCD relief or to carry back part of it to generate a repayment of tax.

Key Point

Unlike relief against total profits, group relief is offset against TTP (i.e. after QCD relief). See pro forma computation.

Exam focus

In the past there have been two types of group relief written test questions that have been set:

(1) More than one company where we would need to establish the group structure and transfer losses in the most tax efficient manner.

(2) Two companies that do not have identical accounting periods.

Exam kit questions in this area:

OT case (section B) question:

- Deutsch Ltd

Constructed response (section C) questions:

- Jump Ltd
- Ash Ltd
- Long Ltd and Road Ltd
- Lena Ltd, Mekong Ltd & Nile Ltd

Capital gains groups

- Group consists of parent company plus 75% subsidiaries.
- Unlike group relief the 75% requirement only applies to the ordinary share capital.
- The subsidiaries can be 75% subsidiaries of 75% subsidiaries but must be effective 51% subsidiaries of the parent company.

Parent

$$| \quad 75\%$$

S_1

$$| \quad 75\%$$

S_2

S_2 is 56.25% (0.75×0.75) subsidiary of parent – therefore all are members of one capital gains group

- The rules allow groups to be established through companies resident anywhere in the world.

- However, in the TX examination, only UK resident companies can take advantage of the capital gains benefits.

Implications of gains group

- chargeable assets transferred at no gain/ no loss between group companies (see below)
- companies can elect for chargeable gains and allowable capital losses to be transferred from one group company to another (see below)
- group ROR (see below).

Assets transferred within the group

- Automatically transferred between companies in the capital gains group at no gain/no loss regardless of the price actually paid.
- Transferee company takes over the asset at cost plus indexation to date of transfer (or December 2017 if transfer occurs later).

Election to transfer chargeable gains or allowable capital losses

- A joint election can be made such that a chargeable gain or current year capital loss can be transferred from one group company to another (for CT computation purposes)
  - provided both were members of the gains group at the time the gain or loss arose.
- Time limit for making the election = 2 years from the end of the accounting period in which the gain or loss occurs.
- Capital losses cannot be group relieved and cannot be set against other profits of the group, however, this election:
  - allows capital losses and chargeable gains to be matched within a group
  - thus maximising the use of capital losses to cover capital gains in other group companies.

Rollover relief (ROR)

- For ROR purposes all the companies within a capital gains group are treated as carrying on a single trade.

- Therefore a qualifying asset can be sold by one company and the gain can be rolled over into an asset acquired by another company in the group making a qualifying reinvestment within the relevant time period.

Exam focus

Exam kit questions in this area:

Constructed response (section C) questions:

- Fogo Ltd and Netta Ltd
- Ash Ltd

13

Tax administration for a company

In this chapter

- Self-assessment.
- Compliance checks.
- Penalties.

Self-assessment

Payment date
 	
• Normal date
• Large company (see below)
	• Nine months and one day after end of AP
	• Four quarterly instalments:
	  on 14th of months 7, 10, 13 and 16 after **start** of AP
	• Based on estimated liability for the year
	• Payments must be reviewed and revised as necessary at each instalment date
	• A company will **not** be required to make quarterly instalments in two circumstances:
	  (1) CT liability is < £10,000
	  (2) Company not large in previous AP, and augmented profits ≤ £10 million (÷ number of 51% group companies)

Payment method	• Payment must be made electronically
Filing date	• 12 months after end of period of account • Must be filed electronically along with copies of accounts • Must be filed using Inline eXtensible Business Reporting Language (iXBRL)
Late payment interest Repayment interest	• Charged from due date • Earned from date paid • Charges and receipts are interest expense/income under the loan relationship rules
Retention of records	• Six years from end of AP

Large companies

- Large companies must pay corporation tax by instalments (see table above).
- A company is large if its augmented profits for the AP > £1.5 million (reduced for short APs).

Augmented profits

TTP	X
Dividends received (Note)	X
Augmented profits	X

Note: exclude dividends from 51% group companies.

Groups of companies

- The £1.5 million and £10 million augmented profits thresholds are reduced if a company has any related 51% group companies.
- The number of 51% group companies is determined at the end of the previous AP.
- Dormant companies are excluded but overseas companies are included.

51% group companies

- Two companies are 51% group companies if:
  - one is a 51% subsidiary of the other, or
  - both are 51% subsidiaries of a third company.
- A 51% subsidiary is one where > 50% of share capital is directly or indirectly owned.
- Companies can only be linked by a corporate parent (i.e. not an individual).

Exam focus

It is important that you have a good working knowledge of the self-assessment rules, and in particular, payment dates of tax.

Exam kit questions in this area:

OT case (section B) question:

- Deutsch Ltd

Constructed response (section C) questions:

- Clueless Ltd
- E-commerce Ltd
- Lucky Ltd
- Lena Ltd, Mekong Ltd & Nile Ltd
- Mixture Ltd

Compliance checks

- HMRC must give written notice of their intention to commence a compliance check (enquiry) into a tax return.
- The time limit to make a compliance check is:

  Where a return is submitted on time:

  - 12 months after the actual submission date.

  Where a return is submitted late:

  - 12 months after 31 January, 30 April, 31 July or 31 October following the actual filing date of the return.

- A compliance check ends when HMRC give notice.
- Company has 30 days to amend the return, if applicable.

Amendments and claims for overpayment relief

- A company may amend its return:
  - within 12 months from the filing date.
- HMRC may amend a return:
  - within 9 months from the date the return is filed.
- A company may make a claim for overpayment relief:
  - within four years from the end of the relevant accounting period.

Determination of tax

- Issued by HMRC when a return is not filed by the filing date.
- Can be issued by HMRC within three years from filing date (i.e. within four years of the end of the period of account).
- Assessment = replaced by the actual self-assessment return when it is submitted.

Discovery assessments, appeals to resolve disputes with HMRC

- Same rules for income tax, corporation tax, capital gains tax, VAT and NIC (Chapter 9).

Penalties

Standard penalties

- Same rules for income tax, corporation tax, CGT, VAT and NIC (Chapter 9).

Other penalties for corporation tax

Offence	Penalty
Late filing of corporation tax return: • Within 3 months of filing date • More than 3 months after filing date Additional penalties: • 6-12 months after filing date • More than 12 months after filing date	• Fixed penalty = £100 (Note) • Fixed penalty increased to £200 (Note) • Additional 10% of tax outstanding 6 months after filing date • Additional penalty increased to 20% Note: Fixed penalties rise to £500 and £1,000 if persistently filed late (i.e. return for 2 preceding periods also late).
Failure to keep and retain required records.	Up to £3,000 per accounting period.

Computation of gains and tax payable

In this chapter

- Chargeable gains.
- Tax payable.
- Chargeable individuals.
- Chargeable gain computation.
- CGT liability – individuals.
- Pro forma – CGT computation 2022/23.
- Capital losses.
- Transaction not at arm's length.
- Connected persons.
- Spouses and civil partners.
- Planning opportunities.

Chargeable gains could be tested in all three sections of the TX examination.

It is therefore essential that you have a sound knowledge of the treatment of capital gains and that you understand the different treatment of gains by companies and individuals.

Chargeable gains

- A chargeable gain arises when:
  - a chargeable disposal is made
  - by a chargeable person
  - of a chargeable asset.

Tax payable

- Companies
  - pay corporation tax.
- Individuals
  - pay capital gains tax.

Chargeable gains

Chargeable persons
- individual
- company.

Chargeable assets
- all assets unless specifically exempt.

Chargeable disposals
- sale
- gift
- exchange
- loss/destruction of asset
- compensation for damage.

Exempt assets
Examples:
- cars
- non-wasting chattels bought & sold for < £6,000
- cash
- wasting chattels (e.g. horses, boats, caravans)
- qualifying corporate bonds (QCBs) and gilts held by an individual
- individual's main residence
- assets held in ISAs.

Exempt disposals
- sale is a trading disposal
- transfers on death
- transfers to charity.

Exam focus

It is vital that you have learnt the key exempt assets, as these represent straightforward marks in the exam and could easily be the subject of an objective test question.

In written questions, you should state that the asset is exempt to score a mark, and not waste any time doing unnecessary calculations.

Chargeable individuals

Individuals are liable to CGT if they are resident in the UK.

Definition of residence is the same as for income tax (see Chapter 1).

Chargeable gain computation

	Notes	£
Gross disposal proceeds	(1)	X
Less: Selling costs	(2)	(X)
Net disposal proceeds		X
Less: Allowable costs	(3)	(X)
Chargeable gain		X

Notes:

(1) Use market value where transaction not at arm's length.

(2) Include legal fees, advertising costs, etc.

(3) Include purchase price and purchase expenses (e.g. legal fees), and any capital enhancement expenditure.

CGT liability – individuals

- Individuals pay capital gains tax (CGT) on their taxable gains for a tax year.

- To calculate an individual's CGT liability:

  (1) Calculate the chargeable gains / allowable losses on the disposal of each chargeable asset separately.

  (2) Consider availability of any CGT reliefs (Chapter 16).

  (3) Calculate the net chargeable gains arising in the tax year
  = (chargeable gains less allowable losses).

  (4) Deduct the annual exempt amount (AEA).

  (5) Deduct capital losses brought forward = taxable gains.

  (6) Calculate the CGT payable.

Pro forma – CGT computation – 2022/23

	£
Net chargeable gains for the tax year (after specific reliefs)	X
Less: AEA (2022/23)	(12,300)
	X
Less: Capital losses b/f	(X)
Taxable gains	X
CGT (10% / 18% x gains in BRB) (20% / 28% x gains above BRB)	X
Less: Payments on account	(X)
CGT payable	X

Due date   31 January 2024

(i.e. 31 January after end of tax year)

CGT payable

- Taxable gains taxed as top slice of taxable income.
- Taxable gains in basic rate band (BRB) = taxed at 10% (18% if residential property).
- Taxable gains falling above BRB = taxed at 20% (28% if residential property).
- In addition, some gains may be taxed at 10% if business asset disposal relief is available (Chapter 16).

Exam focus

Exam kit questions in this area:

OT case (section B) question:

- Albert and Charles

Constructed response (section C) questions:

- Ginger and Nigel
- Mick Stone
- Ruby
- Aurora

Capital losses

Current year losses	Brought forward losses
Must be set off against current year chargeable gains.	Offset after AEA deducted, so AEA not wasted.
Offset before brought forward losses.	
Cannot restrict the offset to preserve the AEA.	

Transaction not at arm's length

- Use market value instead of actual proceeds.
- Applies to:
  - gifts
  - disposals to connected persons (except married couple/civil partnership transfers).

Connected persons

- At TX, an individual = connected with close relatives (i.e. parents, siblings, children).
- Consideration for disposal = Market value.

Spouses and civil partners

For CGT purposes, married couple and civil partnership transfers are treated as follows:

- The connected persons rules are overridden.
- Spouse or civil partner transfers:
  - take place at no gain/no loss
  - regardless of any actual consideration which may have been received.
- The transferor is deemed to dispose of the asset at its acquisition cost
  - i.e. the spouse / civil partner takes over the asset at its original cost.

Exam focus

For CGT purposes you need to know how to deal with transactions between spouses/civil partners and also to be able to suggest simple tax planning opportunities.

Exam kit questions in this area:

OT case (section B) question

- Albert and Charles

Constructed response (section C) question

- Jerome

Planning opportunities

- The ability to transfer assets between spouses/civil partners with no CGT consequences provides a number of opportunities:

  - ensure both spouses/civil partners use their AEAs each year

  - ensure gains are realised by the spouse/civil partner who has capital losses

  - ensure any taxable gains are realised by the spouse who has any basic rate band remaining.

Other CGT planning opportunities

- Delaying disposals until the following tax year can save tax:
  - if the AEA is available in the following year but not the current year
  - if more BR band available in the following year than the current year.
- Selling assets piecemeal across different tax years to utilise more than one AEA will save tax.
- Delaying disposals can also result in the tax being paid at a later date.

Computation of gains: Special rules and shares and securities

In this chapter

- Part disposals.
- Chattels.
- Wasting assets.
- Insurance claims.
- Shares and securities.

Part disposals

Key Point

Where only part of an asset is disposed of the cost is adjusted to reflect the cost of the part sold.

- Cost of part of asset disposed of:

    $$\text{Cost} \times \frac{A}{A + B} \quad \begin{array}{l} A = \text{consideration} \\ B = \text{MV of the remainder} \end{array}$$

- Incidental costs which relate:
    - wholly to the part sold = fully deductible
    - to the whole asset = apportioned as above i.e. A/(A+B).

Exam focus

Exam kit questions in this area:

OT case (section B) question:

- Jorge Jung

Constructed response (section C) questions:

- Mick Stone
- Jerome

Chattels

Definition

Tangible movable property (e.g. painting, jewellery, racehorse, boat, caravan).

Wasting chattels:

- expected life ≤ 50 years
  (e.g. racehorse, boat, caravan)
- exempt from CGT unless plant & machinery on which capital allowances claimed.

Non-wasting chattels:

- expected life > 50 years
  (e.g. antiques, paintings)
- subject to £6,000 rule.

Exam focus

Exam kit questions in this area:

OT case (section B) question:

- Jorge Jung

Constructed response (section C) question:

- Jerome

£6,000 Rule

Sale proceeds \ Cost	£6,000 or less	More than £6,000
£6,000 or less	Exempt	Allowable loss based on deemed gross proceeds of £6,000
More than £6,000	Normal gain computation but restrict the gain to: 5/3 x (Gross proceeds − £6,000)	Normal gain computation

Wasting assets

Wasting assets (life ≤ 50 years)

Chattels
(i.e. tangible and movable)

Not Chattels
(e.g. copyright royalties)

Not eligible for
capital allowances
(e.g. greyhound)

Eligible for capital
allowances (e.g. plant and
machinery used in a trade)

Normal gain computation but
Allowable cost is calculated as:

$$Cost \times \frac{Remaining\ life\ at\ disposal}{Estimated\ useful\ life}$$

Exempt

- Normal gains computation subject
  to £6,000 chattels rule unless a
  loss.
- No allowable capital loss arises as
  capital allowances already given
  relief for loss in CAs computation
  (i.e. fall in value of asset).

Insurance claims

Different treatment depending on whether:

- Asset lost or destroyed.
- Asset damaged.

Assets lost or destroyed

Asset damaged

Shares and securities

Valuation rules

Transaction:	Consideration:
Sale	Sale proceeds
Gift	Market value
Transfer to a connected person	Market value

Market value of quoted shares:

* Mid-price (i.e. average) of quoted prices in SE Daily Official List on disposal date.

Matching rules

Apply where an individual has made more than one purchase of shares of the same class in the same company.

Disposals matched with:

(1) Acquisitions on same day.

(2) Acquisitions in the next 30 days.

(3) The share pool (shares acquired before the date of disposal are pooled together).

Exam focus

Exam kit questions in this area:

OT case (section B) questions:

* Albert and Charles
* Kat Ltd

Constructed response (section C) questions:

* Ginger and Nigel
* Mick Stone
* Ruby
* Luna Ltd

Disposal of shares by individuals

Share pool	30 days

Date of
disposal
↓

(3) (1) (2)

Step 1 Determine the sale proceeds per share.

Step 2 Identify the purchase dates of the shares and using the matching rules allocate the disposal to the time periods above.

Step 3 Compute the gains and losses on disposals of shares from each matching rule.

The share pool

- The share pool contains shares in the same company, of the same class, purchased before the date of a disposal.
- It contains the amalgamated cost of shares acquired.
- The cost of shares disposed of is calculated as a proportion of the number of shares removed from the pool.
- If there is a disposal of shares:
  - in the individual's personal trading company, and
  - the individual is also an employee of that company

  business asset disposal relief (BADR) may be available (see Chapter 16).
- If an individual disposes of unlisted ordinary shares in a trading company:
  - which they had subscribed for on/after 17 March 2016 and held for ≥ three years starting on or after 6 April 2016, and
  - is not an employee of that company investors' relief (IR) is available (see Ch16).

Bonus issues

Definition

Distribution of free shares to shareholders based on their existing shareholding.

For CGT purposes bonus issues are treated as follows:

- Bonus shares are included in the share pool at £Nil cost.
- The bonus shares are not treated as a separate holding of shares.

Rights issues

Definition

Offer of new shares to existing shareholders in proportion to their existing shareholding, usually at a price below the market price.

For CGT purposes rights issues are treated as follows:

- The number of rights shares are included in the share pool, and the cost of the rights shares is added in the cost column in the same way as a normal purchase.

Reorganisations/takeovers

Definition

Reorganisation:
exchange of existing shares for shares of
another class in the same company.

Takeover:
when a company acquires shares in another
company either in exchange for shares in
itself, cash or a mixture of both.

For CGT purposes reorganisations and
takeovers are automatically treated as shown
in the following diagram.

Exam focus

Exam kit questions in this area:

Constructed response (section C) question:

- Luna Ltd

```
              ┌──────────────────┐
              │   Consideration  │
              └──────────────────┘
                        │
            ┌───────────┴───────────┐
            │                       │
   ┌────────────────┐     ┌────────────────┐
   │ Share for share│     │ Cash and shares│
   └────────────────┘     └────────────────┘
```

Share for share
- No CGT disposal at time of takeover/ reorganisation
- Cost of the original shares becomes the cost of the new shares

Cash and shares
- Part disposal of the original shares
- A = Cash received
- B = Market value of new shares
- Gain arises on the cash element of the consideration

CGT: Reliefs for individuals

In this chapter

- Overview of reliefs.
- Business asset disposal relief (BADR).
- Investors' relief (IR).
- Private residence relief (PRR).
- Rollover relief (ROR).
- Gift holdover relief (GR).

Overview of reliefs

- After computing gains on disposals of individual assets consider the availability of reliefs.
- Some reliefs completely exempt a gain from CGT, or reduce the tax payable permanently, others only defer the gain to a later period.

Types of relief	
Permanent reliefs	**Deferral reliefs**
Business asset disposal relief	Rollover relief
Investors' relief	Gift holdover relief
PRR	
Letting relief	

Key Point

- The reliefs are normally applied to the capital gains before deducting capital losses, except business asset disposal relief and investors' relief (see later).

Business asset disposal relief (BADR)

- Only available to individuals.
- First £1 million of gains on 'qualifying business disposals' are taxed at 10%, regardless of the taxpayer's income.
- Any gains above the £1 million limit = taxed in full at 10%/20%.
- Gains qualifying for BADR are set against any remaining BR band before non-qualifying gains.
- The 10% CGT rate is calculated **after** the deduction of:
  - allowable losses, and
  - the AEA.
- Can choose to set losses and AEA against non-qualifying gains first to maximise relief.

  Exception:
  any losses on assets forming part of the disposal of the business.

- Keep gains which qualify for BADR separate from those which do not qualify.
- For 2022/23 disposals, the relief must be claimed by 31 January 2025.
- £1 million = a lifetime limit (partly used up each time a claim is made).

Qualifying business disposals

The disposal of:

- the whole or part of an individual's trading business (i.e. sole trader or partner)
- assets of the individual's or partnership's trading business that has **now ceased**
- shares **provided**:
  - shares = in the individual's 'personal trading company', and
  - the individual = an employee of the company (part-time or full-time).

An individual's 'personal trading company' = where the individual:

- owns at least 5% of the ordinary shares
- which carry at least 5% of the voting rights.

Note that:

- "Part of a business"
  = a "substantial part" which is "capable of independent operation".
- Disposal of assets (i.e. not shares): Relief = not available on investment assets.
- No restriction to relief for shares disposal, if company holds non-trading assets.
- No minimum working hours to satisfy employee condition.

Key Point

The isolated disposal of an **individual business asset** used for the purposes of a continuing trade does **not** qualify.

Qualifying ownership period

- Disposal of:
  - Individual's trading business = business owned for 2 years
  - Shares = individual's personal trading company and employee for 2 years.
- Where a qualifying business is not disposed of but simply ceases:
  - the assets must be disposed of within three years of the date of cessation, and
  - the business must have been owned for two years prior to cessation.

Applying the relief

(1) Calculate the gains and losses on qualifying and non-qualifying assets separately.

(2) Net off losses relating to the qualifying business disposals against qualifying gains.

(3) Offset all other losses and the AEA against non-qualifying gains.

(4) If necessary, deduct any remaining losses or AEA from the qualifying gains.

(5) Tax the gains as follows:
  - qualifying net chargeable gains at 10%.
  - non-qualifying net chargeable gains as normal at 10% or 20% (remember that qualifying gains utilise the BR band before non-qualifying gains). The rates increase to 18% or 28% where residential property is disposed of.

Exam kit questions in this area:

OT case (section B) questions:

- Hali and Goma

Constructed response (section C) questions:

- Ginger and Nigel
- Mick Stone
- Ruby

Interaction of reliefs

- Other specific reliefs (if available) reduce chargeable gains before BADR is considered.
- If also eligible for BADR the remaining gain is taxable at 10%.

Investors' relief (IR)

BADR is only available if:

- the shares are in the individual's personal company (they hold 5%), and
- they are an officer or employee of the company.

Investors' relief is a different relief which extends the same benefit as BADR (i.e. the 10% CGT rate) to certain investors who would not meet the conditions for BADR.

IR applies to the disposal of:

- unlisted ordinary shares in a trading company (including AIM shares)
- subscribed for (i.e. newly issued shares) on/after 17 March 2016
- which have been held for a minimum period of three years starting on/after 6 April 2016
- by an individual who is not an employee of the company.

- IR is subject to a separate lifetime limit of £10 million of qualifying gains.

Exam focus

Exam kit questions in this area:

Constructed response (section C) question:

- Jack and Tom

Private residence relief (PRR)

```
                        ┌──────────┐
                        │   PRR    │
                        └──────────┘
```

Occupied throughout	Occupied for part of period of ownership	Let (part of the property)
Gain exempt	• Calculate gain • PRR: Gain × $\dfrac{\text{Periods of occupation}}{\text{Period of ownership}}$	• Deduct PRR • Then give letting relief if the owner lets part of the property whilst still occupying the remainder Lowest of: (i) £40,000 (ii) PRR element of gain (iii) Gain re letting period

PRR – Periods of occupation

- Actual occupation.
- Deemed occupation.

You may be presented with an individual's personal circumstances and be required to determine the period of ownership of a property which will qualify for PRR.

You should provide brief explanatory notes for periods of deemed occupation, as these will earn marks.

Exam kit questions in this area:

OT case (section B) question:

- Albert and Charles
- Aurora

Deemed occupation

Conditional	Unconditional
• Up to 3 years – any reason • Any period – employed abroad • Up to 4 years – working elsewhere in the UK (employed or self-employed) • Must be actual occupation before and after • Condition relaxed if reoccupation prevented by terms of employment	• Last 9 months of ownership

Rollover relief (ROR)

- Relief for the replacement of qualifying business assets (QBAs).
- The gain arising on the disposal of a QBA is rolled over where the net sale proceeds are reinvested in a replacement QBA within a qualifying period.
- Available to:
  - individual sole traders, partnerships and companies.

Key Point

ROR is the only relief available to companies (see Chapter 17).

Exam focus

Exam kit questions in this area:

Constructed response (section B) question:

- Kat Ltd

Constructed response (section C) questions:

- Mick Stone
- Fogo Ltd and Netta Ltd

Conditions

> Disposal of and reinvestment

in Qualifying asset:
- Land & buildings
- Fixed plant & machinery
- Goodwill (unincorporated businesses only)

Must be used in the trade

within Qualifying time period:
From 12 months before to 36 months after the sale

Effect of relief

Where net sale proceeds are reinvested:

- The full gain on the old asset is 'rolled over' against the capital gains cost of the new asset.
- No tax payable when the old asset sold.

Gain rolled over is:

- deducted from the base cost of the replacement asset, and
- therefore increases the gain on the subsequent disposal of the replacement asset.

Claim for relief

- Within four years from the later of the end of the tax year of:
  - sale, and
  - replacement.
- For a 2022/23 disposal and replacement; by 5 April 2027.

Partial reinvestment of proceeds

Where net sale proceeds are **not** all reinvested:

- The gain that can be rolled over is restricted.
- A chargeable gain arises = **lower** of:
  - the proceeds not reinvested
  - the chargeable gain.
- Taxable on the disposal of the original asset.
- The remaining gain can be rolled over.

Reinvestment in depreciating assets

Definition

Depreciating asset (DA)

- life of ≤ 60 years.

Common examples in the TX examination:

- Fixed P&M
- Leasehold property of ≤ 60 years.

Method of relief

- Conditions and calculation of amount of relief = same as for ROR.
- Method of relief = different.
- Gain not deducted from base cost of new asset.
- Gain is 'frozen' (i.e. deferred) and crystallises on the earliest of:
  - sale of DA
  - date DA ceases to be used in trade
  - ten years from acquisition of DA.
- When deferred gain crystallises:
  - taxed at appropriate rate of CGT at that time (not at the time of deferral).

- Can defer a gain using a depreciating
  asset (for up to ten years) and later
  acquire a non-depreciating asset and
  claim to rollover the deferred gain
  instead (i.e. defer indefinitely until the
  replacement non-depreciating asset is
  sold)
  - provided the deferred gain has not
    previously become chargeable.

Exam focus

ROR may be examined in a question dealing
with either an individual or a company.

Remember that ROR is the only relief
available to companies. It is therefore more
often tested in a corporate situation (see
Chapter 17).

Gift holdover relief (GR)

Key Point

The gain arising on a gift is calculated using the market value of the asset.

GR must then be considered.

Exam focus

Exam kit questions in this area:

OT case (section B) question:

- Jorge Jung

Constructed response (section C) questions:

- Ginger and Nigel
- Jerome

Conditions

- GR applies to gifts:
    - by individuals
    - of business assets.
- Business assets:
    - Assets used in a trade by the donor or used by the donor's personal trading company
      (i.e. donor holds ≥ 5% of shares).
    - Shares in:
        - any unquoted trading company
        - the donor's personal trading company.

      Note: no requirement to work for company.
- For a gift in 2022/23, a joint election is required:
    - signed by both the donor and donee
    - by 5 April 2027 (i.e. within four years from the end of the tax year in which the gift was made).

Effect of relief

- Gain held over i.e. no chargeable gain arises on donor at time of gift.
- The held over gain is deducted from the donee's base cost of the asset.
- The donee in effect takes over the donor's gain which will be taxed when the donee disposes of the asset.
- Higher gain on disposal by donee taxed at appropriate rate of CGT at that time (not at the time of gift).

Sale at undervaluation

Where the asset is sold, but for less than MV, the 'actual consideration' received is ignored:

- The gain is still calculated using MV.

If the actual consideration > donor's cost:

- the excess is immediately chargeable
- the remaining gain can be held over.

The chargeable gain arising now will be:

- taxed on the donor at either 0%, 10% or 20%
- depending on the availability of the AEA, BADR and the level of taxable income.

If the actual consideration ≤ donor's cost:

- full gift holdover relief available
- all chargeable gain held over.

The held over gain is effectively taxed on the donee when the donee disposes of the asset, at the appropriate tax rate in the year of disposal.

Non-business use

- The GR is restricted where there is non-business use of the asset.
- For shares in a personal trading company:
  - the gain eligible for relief is:

    Gain x $\dfrac{\text{MV of company's CBA}}{\text{MV of company's CA}}$

    Where
    CBA = chargeable business assets
    CA = chargeable assets
  - GR is available regardless of whether the individual works for the company.
  - any chargeable gain arising now will be taxed on the donor at 0%, 10% or 20% depending on the availability of the AEA, BADR and the level of taxable income.
  - the held over gain is taxed on the donee later at the appropriate rate when they dispose of the shares.

- If the donor holds less than 5% of the shares (i.e. it is not a personal trading company):
  - for unquoted shares
    - full relief is still available (there is no minimum % holding)
  - for quoted shares
    - GR is not available.

17

Chargeable gains for companies

In this chapter

- Introduction.
- Capital losses.
- Chargeable gain computation.
- Indexation allowance.
- Enhancement expenditure.
- Shares and securities.
- Rollover relief.
- Summary of key differences.

Introduction

- Companies pay corporation tax on net chargeable gains arising in an AP.
- To calculate net chargeable gains:

  Step 1: Calculate the chargeable gains/losses arising on each asset disposed of in an AP

  Step 2: Aggregate the gains/losses:

	£
Gain (transaction 1)	X
Gain (transaction 2)	X
Loss (transaction 3)	(X)
Net gains in period	X
Less: Capital losses b/f	(X)
Net chargeable gains	A

  Step 3: Include the net chargeable gains (A) in the company's TTP.

Capital losses

- Capital losses are set off against gains arising in the same AP.
- Unutilised losses are carried forward and set against chargeable gains of future APs.
- Capital losses cannot be carried back and cannot be set off against any other income of the company.
- See Chapter 11 for further details.

Chargeable gain computation

The individual gains/losses are calculated in the same way as for individuals (i.e. disposal proceeds less allowable expenditure) however:

- the only relief available to companies is rollover relief (ROR).
- indexation allowance is available for companies, but only applies up to December 2017.
- different matching rules apply for shares and securities.

A company's capital gains and losses are calculated according to the principles of CGT but it pays corporation tax and not CGT on its chargeable gains.

Indexation allowance (IA)

- IA is available up to the date of disposal or December 2017 if earlier.
- IA is based on the retail price index (RPI):

  IA = Cost x Indexation factor (provided in the question).

Enhancement expenditure

- Additional capital expenditure is an allowable cost (e.g. improvements such as building extensions).
- IA is given on the enhancement expenditure from the date that expenditure was incurred.
- Separate IA calculations will be required for the original cost and the enhancement expenditure.

Shares and securities

Valuation rules

The valuation rules for shares are the same as for individuals (Chapter 15).

Matching rules

For companies, shares of the same type are matched as follows:

(1) Same day acquisitions.

(2) Shares acquired in the previous 9 days (FIFO basis).

(3) Acquisitions in share pool.

Calculation of gains

- No IA is given on same day acquisitions and purchases in the previous 9 days.
- IA is available on the share pool shares (see below).

The share pool

Use the following pro forma for the share pool for companies:

	Number	Cost	Indexed cost
		£	£
Purchase	X	X	X
Index to next event			X
Purchase	X	X	X
	X	X	X
Index to next event			X
	X	X	X
Sale	(X)	(X)^{W1}	(X)^{W2}
Pool c/f	X	X	X

W1

$$\frac{\text{Number of shares sold}}{\text{Number of shares in pool}} \times \text{Cost to date}$$

W2

$$\frac{\text{Number of shares sold}}{\text{Number of shares in pool}} \times \text{Indexed cost to date}$$

Notes

- Indexation is calculated every time an operative event occurs (e.g. sale, purchase, rights issue or to December 2017 if earlier).

Do not index up before a bonus issue (see below).

Bonus and rights issues

- A bonus issue is not an operative event in the share pool:
  - just add number of shares into pool, £Nil cost.
- A rights issue is an operative event:
  - index up to the date of the rights issue
  - add number of shares and then the cost of shares to both the cost and indexed cost in the pool.

Reorganisations and takeovers

The rules are the same as for individuals (Chapter 15), except:

- Must take account of IA.
- IA should be calculated up to date of takeover, then again when the new shares are sold (or December 2017 if earlier).
- Acceptable shortcut = index from acquisition to disposal date of shares (or December 2017, if earlier).

Exam focus

Exam kit questions in this area:

OT case (section B) question:

- Hawk Ltd

Constructed response (section C) question:

- Luna Ltd

Rollover relief (ROR)

The rules for ROR are the same for companies as they are for individuals except:

- The gain rolled over is the 'indexed gain'.
- Goodwill is not a qualifying asset for a company.
- The key categories of qualifying business assets (QBA) are:
  - land and buildings
  - fixed plant and machinery.
- In particular, note that a freehold or leasehold interest in land and buildings is a QBA, but if the leasehold is for ≤ 60 years on acquisition the gain can only be deferred for a maximum of ten years.
- The claim deadline for companies is within four years of the later of the end of the accounting period in which the asset is:
  - sold, and
  - replaced.

Exam focus

ROR is the only major capital gains relief available to companies. It is therefore more likely to be tested in the examination in a corporate based question.

Summary of key differences

	Company	Individual
Tax paid	Corporation tax	Capital gains tax
AEA	Not available	2022/23 = £12,300
Indexation allowance	Available to date of disposal or December 2017 if earlier	Not available
Capital losses b/f	Offset in full	Offset after the AEA
Shares and securities	Indexed cost column needed Different matching rules	No indexation allowance
Reliefs	Only ROR available Goodwill is not a QBA	Many reliefs are available

Exam focus

You may be required to deal with a chargeable gain computation for either a company or an individual.

It is essential that you are aware of the differences in the way that the gains are calculated.

Inheritance tax

In this chapter

- Charge to inheritance tax.
- Lifetime gifts.
- IHT computations.
- Diminution in value.
- Due dates of payment.
- Exemptions.
- Pro forma – Death estate.
- Married couples and civil partners.
- Lifetime giving.
- Skipping a generation.

Inheritance tax could be tested in all three sections of the examination.

Charge to inheritance tax (IHT)

- Occasions of charge:
    - Lifetime gifts.
    - Death estate.
- Charged on:
    - a chargeable transfer (see later)
    - of chargeable property
    - by a chargeable person.
- Chargeable property:
    - all capital assets / wealth
    - no exempt assets for IHT.
- Chargeable person:
    - individuals.
- Gratuitous intent:
    - transfer must be a gift
    - intention to give asset away
    - not a poor business deal.

Lifetime gifts

* Two types:
  - Potentially Exempt Transfers (PETs)
  - Chargeable Lifetime Transfers (CLTs).

	PETs	**CLTs**	
Definition	Gift by individual to another individual	Gift which is not: • Exempt, or • a PET For TX = gift into a trust	
Chargeable	Only if donor dies within seven years of gift	At date of gift	Additional IHT computation if donor dies within seven years of gift
Tax rates	Death rates	Lifetime rates	Death rates
Tax paid by	Donee	Donee, or Donor (if so; gross up gift for tax paid)	Donee

IHT computations

An IHT charge can arise in three different situations. The computation in each situation is different and must be studied carefully.

(1) Lifetime transfers – IHT on CLTs.

(2) Death – IHT on PETs and additional IHT on CLTs.

(3) Death estate.

In each situation:

- Stage 1: Compute the chargeable transfer.

- Stage 2: Compute the taxable amount.

- Stage 3: Compute the tax.

Stage 1: The chargeable transfer

The first stage of the computation for each situation is always the same; compute the chargeable transfer. For lifetime gifts:

	£	
Transfer of value:		
Value before	X	Diminution in
Value after	(X)	value principle
	—	
	X	
Deduct:		
Exemptions	(X)	See below
	—	
Chargeable transfer	A	
	—	

Order of exemptions:

(1) Small gifts, inter-spouse and civil partner gifts.

(2) Marriage exemption.

(3) AE – current year, then b/fwd.

Diminution in value

Gifts

- IHT uses the 'diminution in value' principle to calculate the lifetime 'transfer of value' (i.e. value by which the donor's estate has been reduced as a result of the gift).

	£
Value of estate before transfer	X
Value of estate after transfer	(X)
Transfer of value	X

- In most cases the transfer of value = value of asset gifted.

- In some cases the fall in value of the estate > value of the asset gifted (e.g. gift of unquoted shares).

Key Point

It is important to appreciate the difference here between CGT and IHT.

- For CGT purposes:
    - a gift is always valued at the market value of the asset gifted, at the time of the gift.

Stage 2: Calculating the taxable amount

Stage 2 is also the same for each situation. However, the calculation of the available nil rate bands (NRBs) differs.

	£
Chargeable transfer	A
Less:	
Available NRBs	(X)
Taxable amount	X

Nil rate bands

- For lifetime gifts – lifetime tax:
  - Use NRB in tax year of gift.
- For lifetime gifts – death tax:
  - Use NRB in tax year of death.
- For death estate:
  - Use NRB in tax year of death
  - Calculate the available residence nil rate band (RNRB).

- The NRBs for earlier tax years will be provided in the examination where needed.

Exam focus

Exam kit questions in this area:

OT case (section B) questions:

- Roman
- Afiya

Constructed response (section C) questions:

- Jack and Tom
- Aurora
- Kendra Older
- Marcus
- Lebna and Lulu

Chapter 18

Stage 3: Calculating the tax

1 – Lifetime tax on CLT
(example – gift in 2008/09)

	£	£
Chargeable transfer (A)		222,000
Less:		
NRB at gift (2008/09)	312,000	
Less: CLTs in 7 years		
prior to gift (say)	(170,000)	
NRB available		(142,000)
Taxable amount		80,000
IHT payable:		
(i) at 20% if donee pays tax		16,000
(ii) at 25% if donor pays tax		20,000

If donor pays tax:
Add IHT to value of chargeable transfer (A)
to calculate gross chargeable amount (B)
(£222,000 + £20,000) = £242,000.

Key Point

Note that the donor is primarily responsible
for the lifetime tax due.

2 – Additional tax on lifetime transfers as a result of donor's death (example – death in 2022/23)

Perform the following calculation for:

- each gift (CLTs and PETs) in the seven years prior to death
- in chronological order.

Gift 1 – CLT or PET

	£	£
Gross chargeable transfer (A or B)		365,000
Less:		
NRB at death	325,000	
Less: CLTs and chargeable PETs in 7 years prior to gift 1 (say)	(140,000)	
NRB available		(185,000)
Taxable amount		180,000

	£
IHT payable at 40%	72,000
Less: Taper relief (40%)(say)	(28,800)
Chargeable (60%)	43,200
Less: Lifetime tax paid (say)	(10,000)
IHT payable	33,200

Then perform the same calculation for gift 2 etc.

Taper relief

Years before death	% reduction
Over 3 but less than 4 years	20%
Over 4 but less than 5 years	40%
Over 5 but less than 6 years	60%
Over 6 but less than 7 years	80%

Lifetime tax deduction

- Cannot create a repayment of IHT.

3 – IHT on death estate

Death estate computation:

	£	£
Value of Estate (includes home)		925,000
Less:		
RNRB	175,000	
NRB at death	325,000	
Less: CLTs and chargeable PETs in 7 years prior to death (say)	(280,000)	
NRB available		(220,000)
Taxable amount		705,000
IHT payable at 40%		282,000

Key Point

The RNRB applies when:

- Calculating tax on death estate.
- Chargeable death estate includes a residential home of the deceased that is inherited by the deceased's children/ grandchildren.
- RNRB = lower of MV of home and £175,000.

Exam focus

Exam kit questions in this area:

OT case (section B) questions:

- Roman
- Afiya

Constructed response (section C) questions:

- Aurora
- Kendra Older
- James

Due dates of payment

1 Lifetime IHT

Gift:	Due date:
6 April – 30 Sept	30 April in next year
1 Oct – 5 April	six months after end of month of gift

2 Additional IHT on lifetime gifts due to death

Due date – six months from end of month of death.

Note: always paid by donee.

3 IHT on death estate

Due date – six months from end of month of death.

However, tax is required to be paid with delivery of accounts to HMRC, which may be earlier than due date.

Exemptions

- Annual exemption
- Normal expenditure out of income
- Small gifts relief
  - max £250 per recipient per tax year
- Marriage/Civil partnership exemption
  - £5,000 parent
  - £2,500 grand parent/ party to marriage/civil partnership
  - £1,000 other

1 → IHT on lifetime transfers during lifetime

2 → IHT on lifetime transfers as a result of death

- Transfers between spouses or civil partners = exempt

3 → Death computation

- Taper relief

Annual exemption

- £3,000 per annum.
- Applied to gifts in chronological order.
- Used against PET – even if PET never becomes chargeable.
- Unused amount can be carried forward one year.
- Current year exemption used in priority to brought forward.
- Applied after all other reliefs and exemptions have been applied.

Normal expenditure out of income

- Gift is exempt if made as part of normal expenditure out of income (not capital).
- Must not affect donor's standard of living.
- Must be habitual.
- Level will depend on income of donor.

Exam focus

Exam kit questions in this area:

OT case (section B) question:

- Afiya
- Lebna and Lulu

Constructed response (section C) questions:

- Aurora
- Marcus

Exam focus

Exemptions are likely to feature in an IHT computation – it is important that you can identify when they are available and how they are applied.

Pro forma – Death estate

	Notes	£
Land and buildings		X
Less: Mortgage	(a)	(X)
		X
Car		X
Life insurance proceeds	(b)	X
Cash and bank accounts (including ISAs)		X
All other assets owned by deceased		X
Debts due to deceased		X
		X
Less: Outstanding debts	(c)	(X)
Funeral expenses		(X)
		X
Less: Exempt legacies	(d)	(X)
Chargeable estate		X
Inheritance tax payable		X

Paid by: Executors = personal representatives

Tax on death estate is usually suffered by:

- the residuary legatee (i.e. recipient of 'the rest' of the death estate)
- not those receiving specific gifts.

Notes

(a) Repayment and interest-only mortgages.

(b) Use the insurance policy proceeds, not the market value at the date of death.

(c) Outstanding debts payable by the deceased and incurred for valuable consideration (e.g. outstanding bills, other taxes due: IT, CGT, VAT). Not gambling debts (unless legally enforceable, e.g. by casinos), nor a promise to pay a friend.

(d) Exempt legacies = legacies to spouse or civil partner.

(e) Funds held in pension scheme = outside death estate.

Key Point

All assets are chargeable
(i.e. no exempt assets for IHT at TX).

Assets that are exempt from CGT
(e.g. cars, gilts, ISAs, PRR, etc.) are not
exempt from IHT.

Exam focus

Exam kit questions in this area:

OT case (section B) question:

- Adana

Constructed response (section C) question:

- Kendra Older

Married couples and civil partners

Transfer of unused NRB

- If the NRB has not been utilised at the time of a person's death, the proportion of the unused NRB can be transferred to the deceased's surviving spouse or civil partner.

- The surviving spouse or civil partner will have the benefit of:

  - that person's own NRB, **and**

  - any unused percentage of the deceased spouse's or civil partner's NRB

  for any tax due at death.

- The unused percentage is applied to the NRB at the time of the surviving spouse or civil partner's death

  - **not** at the date of the first death.

- The same principle applies to the RNRB residential nil rate band. The unused percentage can be transferred to the surviving spouse or civil partner.

- The RNRB is only available for deaths on or after 6 April 2017, so spouses who died before that date have 100% of their RNRB unused.

- The executors of the surviving spouse or civil partner must claim the transferred NRB/RNRB by the submission of the IHT return by the later of:

  - two years of the second death, or

  - three months of the executors starting to act.

- As a result, each spouse or civil partner can leave the whole of their estate to the surviving spouse or civil partner with no adverse IHT consequences.

Exam focus

Exam kit questions in this area:

OT case (section B) questions:

- Adana

- Afiya

Constructed response (section C) question:

- Aurora

Lifetime giving

Advantage of lifetime gifts	Disadvantages of lifetime gifts
• Reduces IHT payable on death as assets gifted during lifetime are removed from the chargeable estate.	• Loss of income and use of the capital asset if given away.
• IHT on lifetime gifts likely to be less than IHT in death estate because:	• IHT is not the only tax that needs to be considered re lifetime gifts:
– IHT = Nil (for a PET), and 20% (for a CLT) if the donor lives for at least seven years	– the impact of CGT is also an important consideration.
– the value of the gift is frozen at the date of the gift, therefore by gifting an appreciating asset during lifetime, if IHT becomes chargeable, it is based on a lower amount	
– lifetime exemptions such as the AE, ME, small gifts exemption and normal gifts out of income are available	
– taper relief is available if the donor lives for at least three years.	

Skipping a generation

- Gifting to grandchildren rather than children avoids a further IHT charge when the children die.

- Such planning requires children to be independently wealthy, so that they have no need for the inheritance.

Exam focus

Exam kit questions in this area:

Constructed response (section C) question:

- James

19

VAT

In this chapter

VAT could be tested in all three sections of the examination.

VAT can be examined in the context of companies or an unincorporated business.

Introduction

- VAT is an indirect tax charged on consumer spending.
- VAT is charged on:
  - a taxable supply
  - by a taxable person
  - in the UK
  - in the course or furtherance of a business.
- Output tax: charged on sales.
- Input tax: incurred on purchases and expenses.

Types of supply

VAT registration

A taxable person is someone who is, or is required to be, registered for VAT.

Compulsory registration	Voluntary registration

• Required when:
   – value of taxable supplies (standard-rated or zero-rated)
   – exceeds the registration threshold (i.e. £85,000)
	• Traders making taxable supplies (standard-rated or zero-rated) can register at any time

Compulsory registration

Historic turnover test	Future Test
• Taxable supplies in the last 12 months exceed £85,000	• Taxable supplies in the next 30 days in isolation are expected to exceed £85,000
• Perform test at the end of each month	• Perform test constantly
Inform HMRC:	
• Within 30 days of the end of the month in which the threshold is exceeded	• By the end of the 30 day period in which the threshold is expected to be exceeded
Registered from:	
• First day of the second month after the taxable supplies exceeded the threshold	• From the start of the 30 day period
• An agreed earlier date	
If taxable supplies are wholly zero-rated there is an exemption from compulsory registration	

Exam focus

Exam kit questions in this area:

OT case (section B) questions:

• Candy Apple and Sugar Plum

• Ardent Ltd

Constructed response (section C) question:

• Smart Ltd

Voluntary registration

Advantages	Disadvantages
• Input tax recoverable	• Output tax charged on sales:
• If making zero-rated supplies:	– if make standard-rated supplies to customers who are not VAT registered will be an additional cost to them
– VAT returns will show VAT repayable	– may affect competitiveness
– can register for monthly returns to aid cash flow	• VAT administration burden
• Avoids penalties for late registration	
• May give the impression of a more substantial business	

Exam focus

Exam kit questions in this area:

OT case (section B) question:

• The Whitlock sisters

VAT groups

- Membership

  - Voluntary.

  - By any UK companies under common control.

- Consequences

  - Representative member responsible for accounting for VAT.

  - No VAT on intra-group sales.

  - Only one VAT return to prepare.

  - All members jointly/severally liable for group VAT.

Exam focus

Be prepared to explain whether or not a company should be included in a VAT group.

Deregistration

Compulsory deregistration	Voluntary deregistration
• When cease to make taxable supplies Inform HMRC: • Within 30 days of ceasing to make taxable supplies Deregistered from: • Date of cessation	• If value of expected taxable supplies in the next 12 months will not be > £83,000 • At any time when above test satisfied • Date of request for deregistration, or • An agreed later date

- Consequences of deregistration
  - deemed to make a supply of business assets held at date when cease to be a taxable person (e.g. capital items, trading inventory).
  - exclude items if no input tax reclaimed on them (e.g. cars purchased with private use).
  - no output tax charge if VAT on deemed supply is ≤ £1,000.

Tax point

- The tax point is the date that goods/services are supplied.
- Determines:
  - the VAT return period in which the supply is accounted for
  - the rate of VAT (important where there is a change in rate or a change in the classification of a supply).

Basic Tax Point

Goods: Date goods are available	Services: Date services are completed

Basic tax point is changed to

Earlier Date If payment made, or invoice issued before basic tax point	Later Date If invoice is issued within 14 days after basic tax point and an earlier ATP has not already arisen
Actual tax point (ATP): · Date of payment invoice	Actual tax point: · Date of invoice

Exam focus

Exam kit questions in this area:

OT case (section B) questions:

- The Whitlock Sisters
- Knight Ltd

Constructed response (section C) question:

- Smart Ltd

VAT returns

- Normally quarterly.
- If receive VAT repayments can elect for monthly returns.
- VAT payable
  = (Total output tax less total input tax).
- All businesses must:
  - file the return online, and
  - pay electronically
  - within one month and seven days of the end of the VAT period.

- VAT-inclusive amounts:
  - VAT
    = Gross amount x 20/120 (or 1/6)

  - Net amount
    = Gross amount x 100/120.

Output VAT

Value of supply

- Consideration in money
  - trader's VAT-exclusive selling price less the amount of any discounts applied.
- Gifts of inventory and non-current assets:
  - Replacement value.
- Certain gifts are not taxable supplies:
  - goods which cost ≤ £50 per customer, per year, and
  - any number of business samples and gifts of services (to employees or customers).
- Goods for own use:
  - Replacement value if purchased for business purposes (no output VAT if purchased for private purposes).

Relief for impairment losses

- Relief available where:
  - Output VAT in respect of an outstanding debt has been accounted for and paid by the supplier.
  - The supplier has written the debt off in the accounts as irrecoverable.
  - Six months has elapsed since the debt was due for payment.
- Claim the relief as input VAT on the VAT return.

Exam focus

Exam kit questions in this area:

OT case (section B) question:

- Knight Ltd
- Glacier Ltd (Specimen CBE)

Constructed response (section C) questions:

- Garfield
- Zia

Transfer of a going concern (TOGC)

- Transfer of a business is not treated as a taxable supply for VAT purposes, therefore:
  - no output VAT charged on assets transferred by seller
  - no input VAT recoverable by purchaser.
- Conditions:
  - business transferred as a going concern
  - no significant break in trading
  - to a taxable person (VAT registered or liable to become VAT registered)
  - same type of trade carried on after the transfer.

- The transferee may:
  - take over VAT registration of the transferor, but
  - if the VAT number is taken over, also inherits the transferor's VAT liabilities.
- Where there is a transfer of a business which does not meet the VAT TOGC conditions:
  - VAT must be charged on the individual assets transferred.

Input VAT

- Conditions to reclaim input VAT:
  - Must be taxable person when incurred
    (exception = pre-registration VAT).
  - Supply must have been to the person making the claim.
  - Supply must be properly supported, normally by VAT invoice.
  - Goods/services must be used for business purposes.
- No distinction between capital and revenue expenditure
  - input VAT is recoverable on the purchase of capital assets as well as revenue expenditure.

Irrecoverable input VAT

- Business entertainment
  - Includes hospitality of any kind (e.g. food, drink, accommodation).
  - Excludes entertaining overseas customers and staff entertainment.
- Cars
  - Purchase – only recoverable if used 100% for business.
  - Leasing – if partly used for private purposes, only 50% of VAT on leasing charge recoverable.
  - Car expenses – provided some business use, 100% recoverable.
  - If input VAT is not recovered on purchase, no output VAT is charged on disposal.

- Fuel – Input tax 100% recoverable even if private fuel provided. Output VAT chargeable on:
  - fuel reimbursed in full
    - amount reimbursed
  - not reimbursed at all
    - fuel scale charge
  - partially reimbursed
    - not examinable.
- Private use
  - input VAT cannot be claimed on goods or services not used for business purposes
  - an apportionment is made for partial private use.
- Goods for own use:
  - input VAT recoverable if purchased for business purposes (and output VAT is due as above)
  - input VAT not recoverable if purchased for private purposes (and no output VAT is due).

Key Point

Where VAT is not recoverable on capital expenditure (e.g. purchase of a car), capital allowances are claimed on the VAT-inclusive cost.

Exam focus

Exam kit questions in this area:

OT case (section B) question:

- Knight Ltd
- Glacier Ltd (Specimen CBE)

Constructed response (section C) questions:

- Garfield
- Zia

Pre-registration input VAT

Conditions to reclaim input VAT:

Goods	Services
• Acquired in the four years before registration, and • Still held at date of registration	• Supplied in the six months before registration

Special accounting schemes

- Three special schemes aimed at small businesses.

Cash accounting scheme

Operation	Conditions	Advantages
• VAT accounted for on cash payments and cash receipts	• Taxable turnover ≤ £1,350,000 • VAT payments and returns must be up to date • Must leave the scheme if taxable turnover > £1,600,000	• Do not pay output tax until receive payment from customer • Provides automatic relief for irrecoverable debts

Exam focus

Exam kit questions in this area:

Constructed response (section C) questions:

- Silverstone Ltd
- Smart Ltd
- Garfield

Flat rate scheme

Operation	Conditions	Advantages
• Flat rate of VAT applied to total VAT-inclusive turnover (including exempt supplies & VAT) • Flat rate determined by trade sector • Flat rate only used to simplify preparation of VAT return – still need to issue tax invoices	• Taxable supplies for the next 12 months ≤ £150,000 • Businesses are eligible to stay in the scheme until their VAT-inclusive turnover exceeds £230,000	• Reduces administration – do not need to account for VAT on individual purchases • May reduce total VAT payable

Exam focus

Exam kit questions in this area:

OT case (section B) question:

• The Whitlock Sisters

Constructed response (section C) question:

• Zia

Annual accounting scheme

Operation	Conditions	Advantages
• One VAT return prepared a year • Return due: 2 months after end of annual VAT period • Payments on account (POA): – 9 POA due at end of months 4 – 12 – each POA is 10% of VAT for previous year • Balancing payment due with the VAT return • New businesses base POA on estimated VAT liability	• Taxable turnover ≤ £1,350,000 • VAT payments and returns must be up to date • Must leave the scheme if taxable turnover > £1,600,000	• Reduces administration • Regular payments can help budgeting and cash flow

Exam focus

Exam kit questions in this area:

Constructed response (section C) questions:

• Silverstone Ltd

• Garfield

VAT administration

VAT invoices

- Must issue a VAT invoice within 30 days of the date of the supply.
- Can be sent electronically if customer agrees.
- Exceptions:
  - Supplies are zero-rated.
  - Customer is not VAT registered.
- Evidence for reclaiming input VAT.
- Must contain:
  - identifying number
  - date of issue
  - tax point
  - supplier's name, address and VAT registration number
  - customer's name and address
  - description of goods/services
  - for each description:
    - quantity
    - price/item (excluding VAT)
    - rate of VAT
    - rate of discount offered
  - total amount payable (excluding VAT)
  - total VAT payable.
- Less detailed VAT invoices can be provided for supplies valued up to £250.

Exam focus

Exam kit questions in this area:

OT case (section B) question:

- Candy Apple and Sugar Plum
- Glacier Ltd (Specimen CBE)

VAT records

Must keep records of all goods/services received and supplied, sufficient to allow the return to be completed and allow HMRC to check the return.

- Retain records for six years.
- Type of records to retain:
  - copies of VAT invoices issued
  - record of outputs (e.g. sales day book)
  - evidence to support recovery of input tax
  - VAT account.

Discovery assessments and appeals to resolve disputes with HMRC

- Same rules for income tax, corporation tax, capital gains tax, VAT and NIC (Chapter 9).

VAT penalties

- Standard penalty applies in the same way for income tax, CGT, corporation tax and VAT.
- Depends on the behaviour of the taxpayer (Chapter 9).
- Errors in VAT returns can give rise to
  - Default interest, and
  - Standard penalty for the submission of an incorrect VAT return.
- Specific penalty relating to VAT is:
  - the default surcharge (see below).

Exam focus

Exam kit questions in this area:

OT case (section B) question:

- Knight Ltd
- Glacier Ltd (Specimen CBE)

Constructed response (section C) questions:

- Tardy plc

Default surcharge

Arises	• Return submitted late, or	
	• VAT paid late	
First default	• HMRC serve a surcharge liability notice	
	• Specifies a surcharge period:	
	– ending 12 months after the end of the VAT period to which the default relates	
Further defaults	• Surcharge period extended to 12 months after the end of the VAT period to which the latest default relates	
	• If default involves late payment of VAT – Surcharge penalty levied	
Surcharges	**Default in surcharge period**	**% of VAT unpaid**
	First	2%
	Second	5%
	Third	10%
	Fourth and more	15%

Note:

• Surcharge assessments at rates below 10% will not be issued for amounts of < £400.

• Where rate is 10% or more, the minimum surcharge is £30.

Error on VAT returns

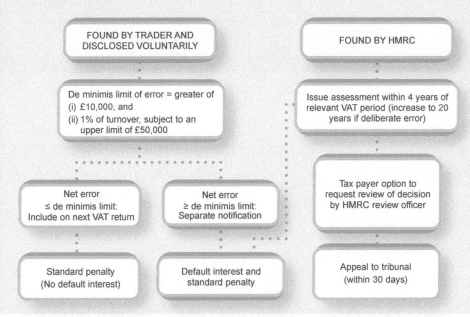

FOUND BY TRADER AND DISCLOSED VOLUNTARILY

FOUND BY HMRC

De minimis limit of error = greater of
(i) £10,000, and
(ii) 1% of turnover, subject to an upper limit of £50,000

Issue assessment within 4 years of relevant VAT period (increase to 20 years if deliberate error)

Net error
≤ de minimis limit:
Include on next VAT return

Net error
≥ de minimis limit:
Separate notification

Tax payer option to request review of decision by HMRC review officer

Standard penalty
(No default interest)

Default interest and standard penalty

Appeal to tribunal
(within 30 days)

Default interest

Arises	• HMRC raise an assessment to collect undeclared/overclaimed VAT
	• Voluntary disclosure of errors exceeding de minimis limit
Charged	• From due date of payment to actual date of payment

Overseas aspects of VAT

Imports of goods

Postponed accounting system applies:

- Importer accounts for output VAT at 20% on VAT return covering date of import
- Can reclaim input VAT subject to normal rules.

Export of goods

All exports are zero-rated supplies.

Exam focus

Exam kit questions in this area:

Constructed response (section C) questions:

- Silverstone Ltd
- Garfield

Supply of services involving an overseas buyer or seller

Where services are supplied to a business customer VAT is charged where the customer is established.

These rules can be applied to B2B transactions involving a UK business as follows:

UK business			Accounting for VAT
Supplies services to	•	Overseas business customer	• Place of supply is overseas.
			• Outside the scope of UK VAT.
Receives services from	•	Overseas business	• Place of supply is UK.
			• Reverse charge procedure:
			– UK business accounts for 'output VAT' at standard UK rate on VAT return.
			– This VAT can then be reclaimed as input VAT.

Exam kit questions in this area:

Constructed response (section C) question:

- Tardy plc

20

Scenario style section C questions

In this chapter

- Scenario question style.
- Comparison of two alternative options.
- Calculation of tax in the margin.
- Multi-tax questions.

Scenario question style

- Scenario style questions are intended to make students think about tax consequences of actions and start to develop higher tax planning skills.
- This style of exam question can include one or more of the following elements:
  - more individual parts to the question with smaller mark allocations
  - more written requirements, rather than just calculations
  - information provided in a less obvious way
  - comparison of two alternative options, with different tax implications
  - calculations of tax at a taxpayer's effective marginal rate of tax
  - combination of more than one type of tax in the same question
  - consideration of tax advantages of certain transactions.

- Note that the actual calculations required tend to be fairly straightforward, however analytic skills are required.

Exam focus

Exam kit questions in this area:

Constructed response (section C) questions:

- Ginger and Nigel
- Mick Stone
- Ruby
- Paul
- Richard Tryer
- Kendra Older
- Jason
- Alimag
- Kat
- Dembe
- Fleur
- Jade

Comparison of two alternative options

- Question 4(a) in December 2012 compared the total tax suffered by taking all the profits from a new company as director's remuneration or as dividends with the total tax suffered as a self-employed individual.

- Question 3(b) in June 2013 required the comparison of disposing of two different warehouses. Part (c) required the comparison of a husband or wife disposing of shares.

- Question 3 in June 2014 required calculating CGT with and without the application of reliefs.

- Question 31 in September 2016 and September/December 2017 required the calculation of the tax saving as a result of a change in the method of extracting income from a company.

- Question 31 in March/June 2018 involved the calculation of the revised tax costs for an individual and a company if a different method of profit extraction was used.

- Question 31 in September/December 2018 tested whether it was preferable to purchase an investment property through a company or personally.

- Question 32 in March/July 2020 requested a calculation of the extra income tax payable if new employment was taken up compared to the existing employment.

- Question 31 in March/June 2021 tested whether there would be a tax saving if a business was run as a sole trader instead of as a company.

- These questions also involved the consideration of different taxes in relation to the same scenario, such as IT, NICs and CT.

- A comparative scenario may ask you to look at the after tax net costs, rather than just the tax cost of the alternatives.

Calculation of tax in the margin

- Question 2(d) in June 2010 required students to calculate the additional IT and NIC due on additional remuneration paid to a director.

- Question 4 in December 2010 required students to calculate the IT and NICs due on both a company car and additional director's remuneration.

- Question 1(c) in December 2011 required students to calculate the income tax reductions for two taxpayers, if further personal pension contributions were paid by one and company car contributions allocated more favourably for the other.

- Question 31 in March/June 2017 required the calculation of the reduction in PAYE payable. In order to answer this requirement quickly it was essential to recognise that the taxpayer was currently in the higher rate band.

- Question 31(c) in September/December 2021 required a calculation of the saving of IT and NICs if the taxpayer undertakes four tax planning measures.

- Although these questions could be answered by preparing full tax computations

    - you are expected to calculate the answers using the individuals' marginal rates of tax

    - the marks (and therefore time available) were allocated accordingly.

- 'Working in the margin' is an important skill in taxation you need to be able to

    - identify whether an individual is a basic, higher or additional rate taxpayer, and

    - calculate the tax on additional income at the appropriate rate.

    This is the only way to achieve the marks in the time available.

Multi-tax questions

- In the past more than one tax has been examined but usually as independent parts of a question.

- Some of the comparison of two alternative option questions however involve IT, NICs and CT.

- Question 5 in June 2013 was unusual as it required the IHT, IT and CGT liabilities of a father and son from just one set of information.

- Question 5(b) in June 2014 required consideration of both CGT and IHT in relation to the same gift.

- Question 31 in September/December 2020 required consideration of both IHT and CGT in relation to three properties.

Tips for success

- Stop and think before writing your answer.

- Make sure you are clear as to what the examining team is asking you to do and that you have identified the simplest way to calculate it.

- Make sure you have spotted all the information the examining team has given you. For example, in Q4 December 2012, the examining team provided the figure for director's remuneration after allowing for employer's class 1 NIC, and since all the profits were withdrawn, the class 1 NIC figure was the difference between the profits and the director's remuneration. Equally, the figure for dividends after allowing for corporation tax was given and therefore the corporation tax liability was the balancing figure. Both these figures could be calculated from the information given, but this would waste valuable time.

- Where there are a number of small parts to a question:
  - make sure you plan your time well, and
  - attempt all parts of the question.

- Lots of requirements can help to provide advice on your approach to the answer:
  - they should be seen as guidance on what to cover, and
  - the requirements are usually very clear, and not misleading.

- Play close attention to any guidance provided by the examining team regarding how to approach the question and which calculations to include.

- Use common sense
  - look at the mark allocation and think about your approach accordingly.

- A two mark question:
    - usually requires 2 or 4 key points/ steps
    - should only take 3-4 minutes
    - should not generate a page of answers!
- Do not waste time doing unnecessary calculations.
- Short workings can appear on the face of the computation.
- Make sure answers are easy to follow and easy to mark.
- Use headings for each separate part of your answer, especially different taxes, and do not try to combine your calculations into one.
- Draw conclusions where you are asked to – not doing so can miss a mark even if your calculations are correct.

Index